Income Tax for the Layman

Income Tax Simplified for Common Man

CA. LOKESH AGARWAL
CA. SHEKHAR AGARWAL

TABLE OF CONTENTS

Foreword 1

Income tax can often feel overwhelming, especially for those without a background in finance. In Income Tax for the Layman: A Simplified Approach to Income Tax Concepts, CA Lokesh Agarwal and CA Shekhar Agarwal have created a guide that simplifies the subject, making it accessible to everyone.

The book is structured in a way that breaks down complex tax concepts into straightforward explanations, allowing readers to easily grasp even the most detailed aspects.

What sets this book apart is the authors' evident dedication and hard work. Their commitment to making tax concepts understandable for all is apparent throughout, turning a traditionally complicated topic into something relatable and approachable.

This book will be an invaluable resource for anyone looking to gain a better understanding of income tax laws, presented in a way that is both informative and refreshingly simple.

Swapan Kumar Dutta, I.R.S (Retd)
Jyotish Road, Tezpur

Foreword 2

Understanding income tax can be challenging for many, with the rules and regulations often feeling complex and confusing. In Income Tax for the Layman: A Simplified Approach to Income Tax Concepts, CA Lokesh Agarwal and CA Shekhar Agarwal have used a simple and engaging format to make tax concepts easy and enjoyable to learn.

The book is structured in a way that presents each topic in clear, concise sections, making it easy for readers to follow and understand. This straightforward approach ensures that readers can grasp one concept at a time without feeling overwhelmed. The authors use a conversational tone, making it feel as if they are personally explaining each idea to the reader.

What truly stands out is how the authors manage to simplify even the most complex topics. Their dedication to making tax understandable for everyone is evident, ensuring that readers from all backgrounds can follow along and stay engaged.

CA SAURABH CHOUDHARY

Disclaimer

This book, Income Tax for the Layman, is intended to provide general information about the concepts of income tax in India and is for educational purposes only. The information provided herein is not meant to serve as legal, financial, or professional advice. While every effort has been made to ensure accuracy, tax laws are subject to change, and readers are encouraged to consult with a qualified tax advisor or professional before making any financial or tax-related decisions. The author and publisher disclaim any liability for any damages or losses incurred based on the information in this book.

Introduction

A New Way to Look at Taxes: Easy, Engaging, and Empowering

Welcome to the World of Income Tax

Understanding income tax can often feel overwhelming, confusing, and maybe even intimidating. For most of us, tax season is a time filled with uncertainty and stress. But it doesn't have to be this way. This book is here to change that. The purpose of this book is simple: to make understanding income tax as easy as reading a novel. We'll guide you through the process step-by-step, using clear language, relatable examples, and a practical approach that anyone can follow.

Why Should You Care About Income Tax?

Income tax isn't just a financial obligation; it's a key part of your financial health. Knowing how taxes work allows you to take control of your money, minimize unnecessary payments, and ultimately, achieve greater financial security. Whether you're a salaried individual, a small business owner, or a retiree, this book will help you navigate the rules of taxation in India so that you can make informed decisions.

INCOME TAX FOR THE LAYMAN

The Journey We'll Take Together

Think of this book as your personal guide to understanding the world of taxes. We'll start with the basics—like why we pay taxes and what it means for you. From there, we'll move on to more specific topics, like how your salary, house property, or business income is taxed. Along the way, you'll learn how to take advantage of exemptions and deductions, how to compute your income accurately, and how to reduce your tax liability legally.

By the end of this book, you'll not only understand the tax system but also feel empowered to handle your own taxes with confidence.

A Book Written for You, the Common Man

This book is written specifically for people who are not tax experts. If you've ever felt lost during tax season, this book is for you. If you've ever wondered whether you're paying more tax than you should, this book will show you how to save. Each chapter is designed to build on the previous one, creating a smooth and logical flow. You don't need any prior knowledge of taxes to get started—just an open mind and a desire to learn.

What You'll Learn

Here's a quick look at what you can expect to learn:

- **The Basics of Income Tax**: What is income tax, and why do we pay it?
- **Types of Income**: How different income sources—like salary, house property, and business income—are taxed.
- **Deductions and Exemptions**: How to reduce your tax liability by claiming deductions and exemptions.
- **Rebates**: Tax reliefs available for those with lower incomes.
- **Filing Your Return**: A step-by-step guide to filing your income tax return and verifying it correctly.

Why This Book is Different

Unlike most tax guides, this book is designed to make taxes easy and relatable. We'll explain technical terms in simple language, avoid unnecessary jargon, and provide you with practical tips that you can apply immediately. By using real-life examples and relatable scenarios, we aim to demystify the tax process and make it as clear and understandable as possible.

Your Financial Health Matters

The goal of this book is not just to help you understand taxes—it's to help you feel more in control of your financial future. Taxes are an important part of managing your money, and knowing how they work puts you in the driver's seat. By the time you finish this book, you'll have the knowledge to make smart financial decisions, save on taxes, and avoid common mistakes.

Ready to Get Started?

Let's dive into the world of income tax together. Don't worry—this is not a crash course in taxation, but a journey where you will learn, understand, and gain confidence with each chapter. Let's turn the page and begin the story of income tax, simplified just for you!

What Is Income Tax?

Demystifying the Basics: What You Pay and Why It Matters

1.1 Introduction to Income Tax

Income tax is one of the most essential aspects of a country's financial system, and it directly impacts individuals, businesses, and the government. But for many, it remains a mystery: Why do we pay it? How much should we pay? What is taxed?

In simple terms, **income tax** is a tax you pay on your income. It is a contribution to the government that allows it to fund public services like healthcare, education, infrastructure, and law enforcement. This means that a part of the money you earn is set aside for the greater good of the society in which you live.

1.2 The Concept of Income Tax

At its core, income tax is straightforward. Every person, whether they are earning a salary, running a business, or making money through investments, contributes a portion of their earnings to the government. The tax is calculated based on the income you earn in a year, and higher income typically means paying a higher percentage in tax.

Key Point: In India, the amount of income tax you pay depends on your income bracket (also known as tax slabs), which we'll explore in a later chapter.

1.3 Types of Income Tax

Income tax is broadly categorized into **Direct Tax** and **Indirect Tax**. Here's how they differ:

- **Direct Tax**: This is a tax paid directly to the government by the taxpayer. Income tax is a form of direct tax because it is based directly on the income you earn.
- **Indirect Tax**: This is a tax paid indirectly when you purchase goods or services. For example, the Goods and Services Tax (GST) is an indirect tax you pay when you buy things.

Since we are focusing on **income tax** in this book, we'll deal with **direct tax**, which applies to your income.

1.4 Why Is Income Tax Important?

You might wonder, "Why do I have to give up part of my hard-earned money?" The answer is simple: The government uses income tax to provide services that benefit everyone, including you. From roads to schools to hospitals, income tax helps ensure that the nation runs smoothly.

Here's how your tax money is typically used:

- **Public infrastructure**: Building and maintaining roads, bridges, and public spaces.
- **Healthcare**: Funding hospitals, medical research, and public health programs.
- **Education**: Running government schools, providing scholarships, and ensuring everyone has access to education.
- **Defense and security**: Protecting the country through military, police, and other security services.
- **Welfare programs**: Providing financial assistance to the underprivileged, unemployed, or elderly.

In short, paying income tax is your contribution to the country's progress and development. It's one way of giving back to the society that supports you.

1.5 The Role of Income Tax in Your Financial Life

Apart from its national importance, understanding income tax is critical for your personal financial health. When you know how income tax works, you can:

- **Plan your finances better**: You'll know exactly how much of your income is taxable and how much you can save through deductions and exemptions.
- **Avoid overpaying**: Many people unknowingly pay more tax than they should

because they don't know the tax benefits available to them.

- **Comply with the law**: Filing your income tax return (ITR) on time and correctly ensures you avoid penalties or legal issues.

1.6 Income Tax in India: An Overview

In India, the income tax system is governed by the **Income Tax Act, 1961**. Every year, the government makes changes to the tax system, usually during the **Union Budget**, which affects how much tax you pay. We'll look into these changes and how they affect your tax planning later in the book.

Here's a quick snapshot of how income tax works in India:

1. **Tax Slabs**: Based on your total income, you fall into different tax brackets or slabs. The more you earn, the higher your tax slab and rate.
2. **Filing ITR**: Every individual who earns income above a certain limit has to file an **Income Tax Return (ITR)** to declare their income and pay taxes.
3. **Deductions and Exemptions**: The tax system also provides reliefs in the form of deductions (like investments in tax-saving schemes) and exemptions (like House Rent Allowance, HRA).

1.7 Who Pays Income Tax?

In India, the following people/entities are required to pay income tax:

- **Individuals**: Whether you're salaried or self-employed, if your income crosses the basic exemption limit, you must pay tax.
- **Hindu Undivided Families (HUFs)**: This is a unique tax entity in India, which allows families to pool their income and pay tax as a unit.
- **Businesses and Companies**: All business entities, including small businesses, partnerships, and large corporations, are required to pay tax on their profits.
- **Other Entities**: Trusts, associations, and other organizations also pay tax on their earnings.

By now, you should have a good idea of what income tax is and why it's an important part of your financial life. You also know that paying taxes isn't just a legal obligation—it's a way of supporting your country. In the next chapters, we'll break down how your income is classified and taxed under the Indian system.

Why Do We Pay Income Tax?

Your Share in Building the Nation

2.1 The Foundation of a Nation

Income tax is not just a financial obligation; it's the backbone of a country's growth and development. By paying your taxes, you are directly contributing to the betterment of the nation. Your tax helps the government deliver essential public services, build infrastructure, and maintain the overall security and well-being of the country.

Every rupee you contribute enables the government to carry out its functions, and it is redistributed to serve the public. Without taxes, the government would struggle to provide the basic services we all rely on daily.

2.2 How Your Taxes Are Used

Income tax is one of the primary sources of revenue for the Indian government. It funds a wide range of public services and welfare programs, which improve the quality of life for millions of people. Here are some of the key areas where your taxes are spent:

INCOME TAX FOR THE LAYMAN

1. **Public Infrastructure**
   - Taxes are used to build and maintain roads, highways, bridges, and public transport systems, making it easier for everyone to commute and travel.
   - They also fund projects like electricity, water supply, sanitation, and other essential utilities that make cities and rural areas functional.
2. **Healthcare**
   - A portion of your taxes goes toward the healthcare system, including government hospitals, vaccination programs, and medical research.
   - Health schemes like Ayushman Bharat, which aims to provide affordable healthcare to low-income families, are financed through tax revenue.
3. **Education**
   - Free and subsidized education, including government schools and universities, are funded by tax contributions.
   - Programs that promote literacy and skill development, such as Sarva Shiksha Abhiyan (Education for All), are also powered by tax revenue.
4. **Defence and Security**
   - A significant portion of the budget is allocated to defence, which ensures

the safety and security of the nation from external threats.
- ○ Law enforcement, police, and public safety are funded to maintain peace within the country.

5. **Welfare Programs**
   - ○ Tax revenue supports welfare programs aimed at helping the underprivileged, elderly, disabled, and unemployed.
   - ○ Schemes like the Public Distribution System (PDS) for food security and the Mahatma Gandhi National Rural Employment Guarantee Act (MGNREGA) for job creation are examples of how tax money directly impacts citizens in need.

6. **Government Operations**
   - ○ Taxes help run government departments and agencies, which are responsible for implementing laws, policies, and maintaining public order.
   - ○ Civil servants, including teachers, police officers, and health workers, are paid through the taxes collected from citizens.

2.3 A Personal Contribution to Society

Think of income tax as your personal contribution to the society you live in. Just as you take part in your local community—by helping neighbours, keeping your surroundings clean, or participating in community events—income tax is a larger, financial way of giving back.

While it might seem like a loss to part with your hard-earned money, the taxes you pay make a tangible difference to millions of people. Roads you travel on, schools your children attend, and the healthcare system you rely on—all are funded by taxes. In that sense, paying income tax is one of the most direct ways you can contribute to your country's progress.

2.4 The Legal Obligation

Beyond the moral aspect of paying taxes, there's also a legal requirement. According to the **Income Tax Act, 1961**, any individual or entity that earns income above a specified threshold must pay income tax. Failing to do so can lead to penalties, fines, or even legal action.

The government has set income tax rules and slabs that define how much tax you owe based on your earnings. These rules ensure that everyone pays their fair share, with those who earn more contributing a higher percentage in taxes. By complying with these laws, you are fulfilling your responsibility as a citizen and avoiding potential legal troubles.

2.5 Social Equity: The Redistribution of Wealth

Income tax serves another important function: **redistribution of wealth**. In a country as large and diverse as India, there are significant gaps between the rich and the poor. Through income tax, wealth is redistributed in a way that supports those who need it most.

Higher earners pay more tax, and this revenue is used to fund social welfare programs that benefit the underprivileged. From subsidies on essential goods to free healthcare and education for low-income families, income tax ensures that wealth is more evenly spread across society.

This system helps maintain social balance, reducing the gap between different economic classes, and ensuring that the basic needs of every citizen are met.

2.6 Taxpayer's Pride: Making a Difference

Being a responsible taxpayer should be seen as a matter of pride. When you pay your taxes, you're not only fulfilling a legal duty but also playing an active role in your country's growth. Every contribution counts, no matter how small.

Imagine driving on a newly paved road, knowing that a fraction of your tax money helped make it possible. Or seeing a community hospital being built in a remote village, knowing that the taxes you paid contributed to that project. Paying taxes is a tangible way to support the country's development and help fellow citizens.

Now that you understand why paying income tax is not only a legal obligation but also a moral duty, you can see how your contributions play a role in building a better society for everyone. Taxes allow the government to maintain the services that make our everyday lives smoother, safer, and healthier.

In the next chapter, we'll dive into a key component of the tax system that every taxpayer needs: the **PAN (Permanent Account Number)**, your unique identity in the world of income tax.

Understanding PAN

Your Unique ID in the World of Taxes

3.1 What is PAN?

Your **Permanent Account Number (PAN)** is a unique 10-character alphanumeric code issued by the **Income Tax Department of India**. Think of it as your fingerprint in the financial world. Just as no two people have the same fingerprint, no two individuals or entities can have the same PAN. It's your personal identification for all tax-related matters, and it helps the government keep track of your financial activities.

The format of a PAN looks like this: **ABCDE1234F**, where the first five characters are letters, followed by four digits, and ending with another letter.

3.2 Why is PAN Important?

PAN is essential for anyone who earns income or conducts high-value transactions in India. Here's why:

INCOME TAX FOR THE LAYMAN

1. **Tracking Income**
   Every time you file an income tax return (ITR) or earn income above a certain threshold, your PAN is used by the Income Tax Department to track your earnings. This helps the government ensure that you are paying the correct amount of tax on your income.

2. **Mandatory for Financial Transactions**
   PAN is required for a wide range of financial transactions, including:
   - Filing your income tax return.
   - Opening a bank account.
   - Making large transactions, such as buying property or vehicles.
   - Investing in the stock market or mutual funds.
   - Applying for loans or credit cards.
   - Receiving taxable salary, professional fees, or any other source of income.

   Without PAN, most of these transactions cannot be completed. This makes PAN one of the most critical documents for anyone involved in financial activities.

3. **Prevents Tax Evasion**
   PAN plays a key role in preventing tax evasion. Since PAN is linked to all your financial transactions, the government can easily detect discrepancies between your income and the tax you've paid. If you try to avoid paying taxes by hiding income, the system will flag the mismatch through your PAN.

3.3 How to Apply for a PAN

Applying for a PAN is a simple process, and it's available both online and offline. Here's how you can get your PAN:

1. **Online Application** You can apply for a PAN online through the official websites:
    - **NSDL (National Securities Depository Limited)** or
    - **UTI Infrastructure Technology and Services Limited (UTIITSL)**

The process involves filling out **Form 49A** (for Indian citizens) or **Form 49AA** (for foreigners), providing proof of identity, proof of address, and a passport-sized photograph. You also need to pay a nominal fee. After successful submission, your PAN will be mailed to your address within a few weeks.

2. **Offline Application** You can also apply for a PAN by submitting the same forms at any PAN service center or UTIITSL office along with the required documents. The PAN will be dispatched to your registered address after processing.

3. **e-PAN (Instant PAN)**
    For those who need PAN quickly, the Income Tax Department offers an instant **e-PAN** service. You can apply for this using your **Aadhaar number**, and you will receive a digitally signed e-PAN in just a few minutes. This service is free of charge and convenient for those who need PAN for urgent transactions.

3.4 Linking PAN with Aadhaar

It is now mandatory to link your PAN with your **Aadhaar**. Aadhaar is a unique identification number issued to Indian residents based on their biometric and demographic data. Linking PAN with Aadhaar ensures that your identity is verified across both systems, reducing the possibility of fraud or duplicate PAN cards.

Here's how you can link your PAN with Aadhaar:

1. Go to the Income Tax Department's e-filing website.
2. Click on the "Link Aadhaar" option.
3. Enter your PAN, Aadhaar number, and your name as per Aadhaar.
4. Verify using an OTP sent to your registered mobile number.

Linking your PAN with Aadhaar is a simple process, but it's essential. Failing to link the two may lead to the deactivation of your PAN, which could affect all your financial transactions.

3.5 Situations Where PAN is Mandatory

There are several instances where having a PAN is mandatory. Some of the common situations include:

- **Filing Income Tax Returns**: You cannot file your tax returns without a PAN.
- **Opening a Bank Account**: Every bank in India requires you to submit your PAN when you open an account.

- **Large Financial Transactions**: If you are depositing or withdrawing cash over ₹50,000 in a bank or post office, PAN is required.
- **Purchasing Property or Vehicles**: PAN is mandatory for buying or selling immovable property valued at ₹10 lakh or more, or purchasing vehicles above a certain limit.
- **Mutual Funds, Shares, and Securities**: If you are investing in the stock market or mutual funds, PAN is essential to track your investments and earnings.
- **Receiving Payments**: PAN is necessary if you are receiving professional fees, commissions, or rent above ₹30,000.

3.6 Misuse of PAN: Be Cautious

Since PAN is so crucial for financial transactions, it is important to keep it safe. Here are a few tips to avoid PAN misuse:

- Never share your PAN with untrusted sources or on public platforms.
- Don't leave photocopies of your PAN unattended when submitting for any service.
- Monitor your financial statements regularly to ensure no unauthorized transactions have been made using your PAN.
- If you suspect misuse or loss of PAN, immediately inform the authorities and file a complaint with the Income Tax Department.

3.7 Multiple PAN Cards: Avoid the Pitfall

It is illegal to hold more than one PAN. Multiple PAN cards can lead to tax evasion charges and heavy penalties. If you realize that you hold more than one PAN card, you should immediately surrender the duplicate PAN to the Income Tax Department to avoid any legal consequences.

Conclusion

Your PAN is more than just a number—it's your identity in the world of income tax and financial transactions. Without it, your ability to conduct essential financial activities could be severely limited. By now, you should understand why PAN is so important and how to get one if you don't already have it.

In the next chapter, we'll explore the different **Types of Income and Their Sources**, helping you understand how your earnings are classified for tax purposes.

Types of Income and Their Sources

Know Taxability of Different Incomes

4.1 Classifying Income: The Five Heads of Income

When it comes to calculating your tax liability, understanding the different types of income is crucial. The **Income Tax Act** classifies your earnings under five major heads of income. These categories help the government determine how much tax you owe based on the source of your income.

The five heads of income are:

1. **Income from Salary**
2. **Income from House Property**
3. **Income from Business or Profession**
4. **Capital Gains**
5. **Income from Other Sources**

Each of these categories is taxed differently, and understanding where your income falls will help you file your taxes accurately. Let's dive deeper into each of these.

4.2 Income from Salary

If you are employed and receive a salary, your earnings fall under this category. **Income from salary** includes:

- **Basic salary**: Your fixed monthly or annual pay.
- **Allowances**: Additional amounts provided for specific purposes like **House Rent Allowance (HRA), Leave Travel Allowance (LTA)**, or **transport allowance**.
- **Perquisites**: Non-cash benefits like company-provided accommodation, car, or other fringe benefits.
- **Bonuses and commissions**: Any extra payments made by your employer.

Salary income is taxable based on the **tax slab** applicable to you. Your employer will deduct **Tax Deducted at Source (TDS)** from your salary each month based on your estimated annual income. However, you can reduce your taxable income by claiming exemptions such as **HRA, Standard Deduction**, and other applicable deductions under Section 80C and others (which we'll cover in later chapters).

4.3 Income from House Property

Income from house property refers to any income you earn from owning real estate. This category includes:

- **Rental Income**: If you rent out a house or building that you own, the rent you receive is taxable under this head.
- **Deemed Rental Income**: Even if you own a property and don't rent it out, it may still be considered as generating rental income, depending on certain conditions (e.g., owning more than one property).

You are allowed deductions from this income, such as:

- **Standard Deduction of 30%**: This deduction is allowed to cover maintenance and repairs, regardless of your actual expenses.
- **Home Loan Interest Deduction**: If you have taken a loan to purchase or construct a house, you can deduct the interest paid on the loan (up to ₹2 lakh for self-occupied property under Section 24).

4.4 Income from Business or Profession

If you are self-employed, running a business, or practicing a profession (like a doctor, lawyer, or consultant), your earnings fall under this head.

Types of Income in This Category

- **Business Income**: Any profits from running a business, whether it's a shop, a consultancy, or a service-based company.
- **Professional Income**: If you practice a profession independently (e.g., as a doctor or

lawyer), your income is considered professional income.

Taxation of Business or Professional Income

For businesses and professionals, income is calculated by deducting business-related expenses (like rent, utilities, employee salaries, and operational costs) from the total revenue. You can also opt for **presumptive taxation** if your turnover is below a certain threshold, simplifying the calculation of taxable income.

4.5 Capital Gains

Capital gains refer to the profit you make when you sell an asset like property, stocks, or mutual funds for more than what you paid for it. Capital gains are categorized into:

- **Short-term capital gains (STCG)**: If you sell an asset within a short period (e.g., property within 24 months or shares within 12 months), the profit is considered short-term capital gains.
- **Long-term capital gains (LTCG)**: If you hold the asset for a longer duration before selling it, the profit is categorized as long-term capital gains.

- **Short-term gains** are added to your total income and taxed based on your applicable tax slab.
- **Long-term gains** on certain assets like equity shares and mutual funds are taxed at a lower rate (10% without indexation if gains exceed ₹1 lakh). For property, LTCG is taxed at 20% with indexation benefits, which adjust the purchase price to account for inflation.

Exemptions on Capital Gains

To reduce your tax liability, you can reinvest the gains in certain assets to claim exemptions under **Section 54** (for property) or **Section 54EC** (for bonds).

4.6 Income from Other Sources

If your income doesn't fall under the first four categories, it will be taxed under **Income from Other Sources**. This is a catch-all category and includes:

- **Interest Income**: Interest from savings accounts, fixed deposits (FDs), or bonds.
- **Dividends**: Any dividends received from investments in shares or mutual funds.
- **Lottery winnings or gifts**: Any income from gambling, lotteries, or gifts above ₹50,000.

- **Pension**: Pension received from a former employer is also taxable under this head.

Taxation of Income from Other Sources

Income from other sources is generally taxed at your applicable tax slab rate. However, certain incomes, like winnings from lotteries or gifts, are taxed at a flat rate of 30%.

Understanding how your income is classified is the first step toward managing your tax liabilities effectively. Whether you're earning a salary, rent, or capital gains, each type of income has specific tax rules. Knowing these will help you plan your taxes and take advantage of deductions and exemptions where applicable.

In the next chapter, we'll dive deeper into **Income from Salary**, explaining its components, exemptions, and how to reduce your taxable salary through legitimate means.

Income from Salary

Breaking Down Your Paycheck

5.1 Introduction to Salary Income

If you're an employee earning a monthly salary, your income is classified as **Income from Salary**. This is often the most straightforward form of income, but the way it's taxed can vary based on your salary components. Salary income includes not only the amount credited to your bank account but also other benefits like allowances and perks provided by your employer.

The Income Tax Act treats salary income as taxable after certain exemptions and deductions, which are essential for reducing your overall tax liability.

5.2 Components of Salary Income

Your salary isn't just the fixed amount you receive each month—it's made up of various components. Understanding these components will help you figure out which parts are taxable, and which are exempt.

Basic Salary

- **Basic salary** is the fixed portion of your salary and typically forms the largest part of your total earnings. This amount is fully taxable.

- Your employer calculates other benefits, such as bonuses or allowances, based on your basic salary.

Allowances

Allowances are additional payments made to cover specific expenses like rent, travel, or medical costs. Some allowances are fully taxable, while others are partially or fully exempt from tax. Here are the most common types of allowances:

- **House Rent Allowance (HRA)**:
  HRA is provided to cover rent expenses, and it's one of the most significant exemptions salaried individuals can claim. If you live in a rented home, you can claim a partial HRA exemption. The exempt amount is calculated based on:
  - The actual HRA received.
  - 50% of your basic salary if you live in a metro city (40% if in a non-metro).
  - Rent paid minus 10% of your basic salary.

  Note: You cannot claim HRA exemption if you live in your own house.

- **Leave Travel Allowance (LTA)**:
  LTA is paid to cover travel expenses incurred while on leave. You can claim an LTA exemption twice in a block of four years for domestic travel (airfare, train fare, etc.).

However, it only covers travel costs, not food, accommodation, or other expenses.

- **Conveyance Allowance**:
  This allowance is given to cover transportation costs. A standard deduction of ₹1,600 per month (₹19,200 annually) was previously allowed, but after the introduction of the **Standard Deduction** (explained below), this allowance is no longer separately exempt.

- **Medical Allowance**:
  Employees may receive a medical allowance to cover their healthcare expenses. However, after the Standard Deduction was introduced, medical allowances are now fully taxable unless reimbursed for actual medical bills up to ₹15,000 per annum.

Perquisites (Perks)

Perquisites are benefits or perks provided by your employer in addition to your salary. These perks can be monetary or non-monetary and are often taxable. Common taxable perquisites include:

- **Rent-free accommodation**: If your employer provides you with accommodation, the value of the benefit is added to your taxable salary.
- **Company car**: If you use a company-provided car for personal purposes, the value of this benefit is considered taxable income.
- **Employer contributions to Provident Fund (PF)** beyond the exempt limit: If your

employer contributes more than ₹2.5 lakh annually to your PF, the excess amount is taxable as perquisite.

5.3 Deductions from Salary Income

While a significant portion of your salary is taxable, there are several deductions you can claim to reduce your overall tax burden. Understanding and using these deductions wisely can result in significant savings.

Standard Deduction

The **Standard Deduction** is a flat amount that is automatically deducted from your salary income to reduce your taxable income. As of the latest tax regulations, the Standard Deduction is ₹50,000 annually. This deduction replaces earlier allowances like medical reimbursement and conveyance allowance.

Professional Tax

If your state imposes a **professional tax** (a small amount deducted by your employer), you can claim this as a deduction from your salary. The maximum professional tax deduction allowed is ₹2,500 annually.

5.4 Minimizing Tax on Salary Income Through Exemptions

Knowing how to claim exemptions on allowances can significantly lower your tax liability. Here's how you

CA. Lokesh Agarwal | CA. Shekhar Agarwal
can make the most of the exemptions available for
your salary:

How to Claim HRA Exemption

To claim HRA exemption, you need to provide your
employer with rent receipts or your landlord's PAN
if the rent exceeds ₹1 lakh per annum. This
exemption can result in significant tax savings,
especially in metro cities where rent is typically
higher.

Leave Travel Allowance (LTA) Exemption

To claim LTA exemption, you need to submit travel
tickets and proof of travel to your employer.
Remember that LTA can only be claimed for travel
expenses within India, and the benefit is available
twice in a block of four years.

Perquisites

If your employer provides perquisites like a car or
housing, it's essential to understand which of these
are taxable. Some perks, such as medical
reimbursements up to ₹15,000 (if applicable), can be
claimed as exempt if supported by actual bills.

5.5 Provident Fund (PF) Contributions

If you are a salaried employee, your employer likely
contributes to a **Provident Fund (PF)** on your
behalf. This amount is automatically deducted from
your salary each month and saved for your

retirement. Here's how PF contributions affect your taxes:

- **Employee Contribution**: Your contributions to the **Employees' Provident Fund (EPF)** qualify for a deduction under **Section 80C**, up to the limit of ₹1.5 lakh annually.
- **Employer Contribution**: The employer's contribution to your PF is tax-free up to 12% of your basic salary. Any contribution beyond this limit is taxable as part of your salary.

5.6 Filing Income Tax Returns as a Salaried Employee

If your only source of income is salary, filing your Income Tax Return (ITR) is relatively straightforward. Here are the key steps:

1. **Form 16**: Your employer will provide you with **Form 16**, which summarizes your total salary, deductions, and the TDS deducted by your employer.
2. **Filing ITR-1**: Salaried individuals with income up to ₹50 lakh and no business income can file **ITR-1 (Sahaj)**. This form is easy to fill and is available on the Income Tax e-filing portal.
3. **Claiming Deductions and Exemptions**: Make sure to claim all applicable deductions (like **Section 80C, Standard Deduction**)

and exemptions (like **HRA**, **LTA**) when filing your return.

Conclusion

Salary income is the most common form of income for many taxpayers, but it's essential to understand how each component of your salary is taxed. By knowing what's taxable, how to claim exemptions, and which deductions apply to you, you can significantly reduce your tax liability. Armed with this knowledge, you'll be better prepared to file your taxes and save money.

In the next chapter, we'll explore **Income from House Property**, focusing on rental income, home loan deductions, and tax-saving strategies for property owners.

Income from House Property

Owning a Home? Know About Tax Liabilities

6.1 Introduction to Income from House Property

If you own real estate—whether it's rented out or self-occupied—your property can either generate income or provide you with tax-saving opportunities. The Income Tax Act treats any income you earn from owning property as **Income from House Property**, which is taxed separately from your salary or business income.

You might think that owning a property and living in it wouldn't generate any income, but the tax law considers both **rental income** and **notional (deemed) income** for certain properties.

Let's break down how house property income is classified and taxed.

6.2 What Qualifies as Income from House Property?

Under the Income Tax Act, any rental income earned from a property—whether it's a house, shop, office, or commercial building—is taxable under **Income from House Property**. Here are the different scenarios where you will be taxed:

Rented Property

If you own a property and rent it out, the rent you receive is taxable. This is known as **Rental Income**, and it's calculated as part of your total income for the financial year.

Self-Occupied Property

If you live in your own house, it is considered **self-occupied**, and no income is assumed from it. However, if you own more than one house, only one can be treated as self-occupied. The other(s) are treated as **deemed to be let out**, meaning you are taxed as though they generate rental income, even if they are not rented out.

Vacant Property

If you own a property and it remains vacant despite being available for rent, it is still treated as though it generates income (deemed rental income), depending on certain conditions. However, if the property was vacant for a part of the year due to lack of tenants, you can claim this as a deduction.

6.3 Taxation of Rental Income

For rented properties, your **Gross Annual Value (GAV)** is the key figure in calculating your taxable income. **Gross Annual Value** is essentially the rent you earn from your property, subject to certain adjustments. Here's how to compute your **Income from House Property**:

1. **Gross Annual Value (GAV)**:
   - This is the annual rental income you receive from the property.
   - If you have not rented the property but it's treated as **deemed let out**, the Gross Annual Value is determined by the local market rent.
2. **Municipal Taxes**:
   - Municipal taxes (property tax) paid by you can be deducted from the Gross Annual Value. Only taxes that have been paid during the year can be claimed as a deduction.
3. **Net Annual Value (NAV)**:
   - The Net Annual Value is calculated as **GAV minus municipal taxes paid**.
4. **Standard Deduction**:
   - A flat **30% deduction** is allowed on the **Net Annual Value**. This is meant to cover repairs, maintenance, and other property-related expenses, and it is allowed regardless of your actual expenses.
5. **Interest on Home Loan (Section 24)**:
   - If you've taken a **home loan** for purchasing, constructing, or renovating your property, you can deduct the **interest** paid on the loan from your taxable income. For a **self-occupied property**, this deduction is capped at ₹2 lakh per annum. For rented properties, there's no cap on the interest deduction.

Final Calculation:

The final taxable income from house property is calculated as: **Taxable Income = Net Annual Value – Standard Deduction (30%) – Interest on Home Loan**

6.4 Self-Occupied vs. Rented Property: Key Differences

The tax treatment differs based on whether your property is self-occupied or rented out. Let's break down the differences:

Self-Occupied Property

- **No Income Considered**: You are not taxed on a self-occupied property as it's assumed to generate no rental income.
- **Home Loan Interest Deduction**: You can claim a deduction of up to ₹2 lakh per annum on the interest paid for a home loan under **Section 24**.
- **Principal Repayment Deduction (Section 80C)**: You can also claim a deduction on the principal amount of the home loan repayment under **Section 80C**, up to ₹1.5 lakh annually.

Rented Property

- **Rental Income Taxed**: The rent you receive is added to your total income, and you are taxed based on the applicable income tax slab.

- **No Cap on Interest Deduction**: There's no limit to the interest deduction on a home loan for rented property, meaning you can claim the entire interest paid as a deduction, which helps reduce your taxable income.

6.5 Special Provisions for Second Homes

If you own more than one house property, only one can be treated as self-occupied, while the others are considered **deemed to be let out**. This means:

- For the second home, even if it's not rented out, the Income Tax Department will assume it generates income, and you will be taxed based on the **notional rent** it could have earned.
- You can still claim home loan interest deductions on a second home (without the ₹2 lakh cap), but the rent you could potentially earn (deemed income) will be taxable.

6.6 Home Loan Benefits: Maximizing Tax Savings

Owning a house comes with several tax benefits, especially if you've taken a home loan. Let's explore the deductions you can claim to reduce your tax burden:

Interest on Home Loan (Section 24)

- For a self-occupied property, the **interest paid on the home loan** is deductible up to ₹2 lakh.
- For rented or deemed let-out property, there's **no cap on the interest deduction**. This can be a significant benefit if you're paying substantial interest on your home loan.

Principal Repayment (Section 80C)

- The **principal repayment** on your home loan qualifies for deduction under **Section 80C**, up to ₹1.5 lakh annually. This is available for self-occupied or rented properties, but only if the construction is complete.

Stamp Duty and Registration Charges (Section 80C)

- You can also claim a deduction on **stamp duty and registration fees** (paid when purchasing the property) under **Section 80C**, but this is a one-time benefit, available in the year these expenses are incurred.

6.7 Pre-Construction Interest Deduction

If you've taken a home loan for the construction of a property, you are allowed to claim the **interest paid during the construction phase** as a deduction in five equal installments after the construction is complete. This can help you spread out the deduction over time and maximize tax savings.

6.8 Tax Implications on Selling a Property

If you sell your property, any profit you make is treated as a **capital gain**, which we will cover in detail in the upcoming **Capital Gains** chapter. However, here's a quick overview:

- If you sell the property within **2 years** of purchase, the profit is treated as **short-term capital gains** and taxed at your applicable slab rate.
- If you sell the property after holding it for more than **2 years**, the profit qualifies as **long-term capital gains (LTCG)** and is taxed at 20% with **indexation benefits**.

Conclusion

Owning a house property comes with tax obligations, but also provides many opportunities to save on taxes. Whether you rent out the property or live in it, you can claim deductions on the interest paid on home loans and other property-related expenses. By understanding how house property income is taxed, you can make informed decisions and reduce your overall tax liability.

In the next chapter, we'll look at **Income from Business or Profession**, focusing on how self-employed individuals and business owners can manage their taxes efficiently.

Income from Business or Profession

Running a Business? Know Your Tax Obligations!!

7.1 Introduction to Income from Business or Profession

If you're self-employed, run a small business, or practice a profession like law, medicine, or consultancy, the income you earn is classified as **Income from Business or Profession**. This is different from salary income because you aren't working for an employer but generating your own income through your services or business activities.

Whether you're a sole proprietor, a freelancer, or running a shop or service-based business, understanding how your income is taxed and which expenses you can deduct is crucial to managing your tax liability.

7.2 What Qualifies as Business or Professional Income?

Income from Business or Profession includes any profits you earn from activities where you provide goods or services. This can include:

- **Profits from Business**: If you run a retail shop, online business, or service company, the profits generated from these activities are considered business income.

- **Professional Income**: If you are a self-employed doctor, lawyer, architect, consultant, or freelancer, your earnings are categorized as professional income.

You can also include income from **speculative business** activities (e.g., trading in shares) or **non-speculative business** (e.g., investing in mutual funds) under this head.

7.3 How to Calculate Business or Professional Income

Unlike salary income, where tax is deducted at source (TDS), business or professional income requires you to calculate **profits** after deducting all business-related expenses. Here's how you can calculate taxable income from your business:

Gross Receipts or Turnover

- The total amount you receive from providing services or selling goods is called your **gross receipts** or **turnover**.

Allowable Expenses

To calculate your taxable income, you can deduct any expenses that were incurred in the process of earning your income. These expenses must be necessary for running the business. Some common **allowable expenses** include:

- **Rent for Business Premises**: The rent you pay for your office, shop, or workspace.
- **Employee Salaries and Wages**: Payments made to staff or contract employees.
- **Utilities**: Expenses like electricity, water, and internet that are essential for running the business.
- **Office Supplies and Equipment**: Items like computers, furniture, and other office-related supplies.
- **Travel and Conveyance**: Expenses related to business travel or commuting for professional purposes.
- **Advertising and Marketing**: Costs incurred to promote your business, such as digital ads, print media, or sponsorships.
- **Repairs and Maintenance**: Costs for maintaining office equipment or business premises.

Net Income

Once you've deducted all allowable expenses from your **gross receipts**, the remaining amount is your **net income** (also referred to as profit), which is subject to tax.

Net Income = Gross Receipts – Allowable Business Expenses

7.4 Important Deductions for Business Owners

As a business owner or professional, you can claim several deductions that reduce your taxable income. Some of the key deductions include:

Depreciation on Assets (Section 32)

If you purchase assets like machinery, computers, or office equipment for your business, you can claim **depreciation** on these assets. Depreciation allows you to spread the cost of the asset over several years, reducing your taxable income each year.

Interest on Loans

If you've taken a loan for business purposes (like to purchase equipment, lease property, or expand operations), the interest paid on the loan can be claimed as a deduction.

Bad Debts

If you have any **bad debts**—amounts you're owed but unable to recover—you can claim them as a deduction from your taxable income.

Office Rent and Utilities

The rent you pay for your office or shop, along with expenses for utilities like electricity, water, internet, and phone bills, are fully deductible as business expenses.

Repairs and Maintenance

Any costs incurred to maintain or repair business assets, such as machinery, computers, or office space, can also be deducted.

Travel and Conveyance

Expenses for travel (both domestic and international) that are essential for your business—such as meetings with clients or vendors—are deductible. Even daily commuting for business purposes can be deducted under **conveyance expenses**.

7.5 Presumptive Taxation Scheme (Sections 44AD, 44ADA)

For small business owners and professionals who want to simplify their tax calculations, the government offers a **presumptive taxation scheme**. This scheme allows you to calculate your taxable income as a fixed percentage of your gross receipts, without having to maintain detailed records of expenses.

Section 44AD for Small Businesses

If you are a small business owner with a **turnover of up to ₹2 crore**, you can opt for **Section 44AD**. Under this scheme, your taxable income is assumed to be **8%** of your total turnover (or 6% if receipts are digital), regardless of your actual expenses.

For example, if your business turnover is ₹50 lakh in a financial year, your taxable income under this scheme will be: **Taxable Income = 8% of ₹50 lakh = ₹4 lakh**

Section 44ADA for Professionals

If you are a self-employed professional with gross receipts up to ₹50 lakh, you can opt for **Section 44ADA**. Under this scheme, your taxable income is presumed to be **50%** of your total receipts, again simplifying tax calculations.

For example, if a consultant earns ₹30 lakh in a financial year, the taxable income will be: **Taxable Income = 50% of ₹30 lakh = ₹15 lakh**

Advantages of Presumptive Taxation

- **No need to maintain detailed books of accounts**: You don't have to keep a record of every expense.
- **No requirement for an audit**: Businesses opting for presumptive taxation don't need to get their accounts audited.
- **Simple and easy tax calculation**: A fixed percentage is applied to your turnover or receipts to calculate taxable income.

7.6 Record-Keeping and Compliance

While the presumptive taxation scheme simplifies things, many businesses and professionals need to maintain **detailed books of accounts** if they don't qualify or opt for the scheme. Proper record-keeping ensures you can claim all allowable deductions and comply with tax laws.

What Records to Keep:

- **Invoices and Receipts**: Keep all invoices and receipts related to income and expenses.
- **Bank Statements**: Ensure all your transactions are documented through your bank accounts.
- **Employee Records**: If you employ staff, maintain detailed records of salaries and benefits paid.
- **Inventory**: Businesses that deal in goods should maintain an inventory record of their stock.

7.7 Filing ITR for Business or Profession

Filing income tax returns as a business owner or professional differs from salaried individuals. Here are the key steps:

Forms to File

- **ITR-3**: If you're an individual or HUF carrying on a business or profession, you'll file **ITR-3**.
- **ITR-4**: If you opt for the **presumptive taxation scheme**, you can file the simpler **ITR-4 (Sugam)** form.

CA. Lokesh Agarwal | CA. Shekhar Agarwal
Advance Tax Payments

Unlike salaried individuals, business owners and professionals may need to pay **advance tax** if their tax liability exceeds ₹10,000 in a financial year. Advance tax must be paid in four installments throughout the year.

7.8 Tax-Saving Tips for Business Owners and Professionals

To maximize your tax savings and stay compliant with tax laws, consider the following tips:

- **Maximize allowable deductions**: Deduct all eligible business expenses, including office rent, utilities, and employee salaries.
- **Invest in assets**: By purchasing machinery or equipment, you can claim depreciation deductions over time.
- **Plan for advance tax payments**: Ensure that you calculate and pay advance tax on time to avoid penalties.
- **Consider presumptive taxation**: If your turnover is within the limits, opting for presumptive taxation can simplify your tax filing process and reduce your tax burden.

Conclusion

As a business owner or professional, understanding how your income is taxed and knowing which expenses you can deduct is critical to managing your finances. By keeping accurate records, claiming all allowable deductions, and considering the presumptive taxation scheme, you can minimize your tax liability and stay compliant with tax laws.

In the next chapter, we'll look at **Capital Gains**, focusing on how to calculate and manage taxes on profits from selling assets like property and stocks.

Capital Gains

Selling Assets? Here's How to Save on Taxes

8.1 Introduction to Capital Gains

When you sell an asset—whether it's real estate, stocks, mutual funds, or other investments—at a profit, the amount you earn is known as **capital gains**. Capital gains are considered taxable income and are divided into two categories based on how long you've held the asset before selling it: **short-term capital gains (STCG)** and **long-term capital gains (LTCG)**.

In this chapter, we'll look at how capital gains are calculated, the tax rates applicable to them, and the exemptions and deductions available to help reduce your tax liability.

8.2 Types of Capital Gains

Capital gains are categorized based on the duration for which you hold an asset before selling it. The holding period determines whether the profit is classified as **short-term** or **long-term**.

Short-Term Capital Gains (STCG)

- **Short-term capital gains** arise when you sell an asset within a short holding period.

- For **equity shares and equity mutual funds**, the short-term holding period is **12 months or less**.
- For **real estate and other assets**, the short-term holding period is **24 months or less**.

Tax Rate for STCG:

- If your STCG is from **equity shares or mutual funds**, the gains are taxed at **15%**.
- For **real estate or other assets**, the gains are added to your total income and taxed as per your income tax slab rate.

Long-Term Capital Gains (LTCG)

- **Long-term capital gains** arise when you sell an asset after holding it for a longer period.
  - For **equity shares and equity mutual funds**, the long-term holding period is **more than 12 months**.
  - For **real estate and other assets**, the long-term holding period is **more than 24 months**.

Tax Rate for LTCG:

- **LTCG on equity shares and equity mutual funds**: Gains exceeding ₹1 lakh in a financial year are taxed at **10%** without indexation (no benefit of adjusting the purchase price for inflation).

- **LTCG on real estate and other assets**: Gains are taxed at **20%** with indexation, meaning you can adjust the purchase price for inflation, reducing your taxable gain.

8.3 How to Calculate Capital Gains

The formula for calculating capital gains differs based on whether the gains are short-term or long-term.

Short-Term Capital Gains Calculation

1. **Sale Price**: The amount you receive from selling the asset.
2. **Cost of Acquisition**: The original price you paid to acquire the asset.
3. **Short-Term Capital Gains (STCG) =** Sale Price – Cost of Acquisition – Expenses related to the sale (like brokerage or legal fees).

For example, if you bought shares for ₹1 lakh and sold them a few months later for ₹1.5 lakh, your STCG would be: **STCG = ₹1.5 lakh – ₹1 lakh = ₹50,000**

Long-Term Capital Gains Calculation

1. **Sale Price**: The amount you receive from selling the asset.
2. **Indexed Cost of Acquisition**: The original purchase price adjusted for inflation using the **Cost Inflation Index (CII)**. This reduces

your taxable gain by accounting for the effect of inflation over time.

3. **Indexed Long-Term Capital Gains (LTCG)** = Sale Price – Indexed Cost of Acquisition – Expenses related to the sale.

For example, if you purchased a property for ₹30 lakh in 2010 and sold it for ₹60 lakh in 2024, and the **Cost Inflation Index (CII)** for 2010 is 711 and for 2024 is 348, the indexed cost of acquisition would be: **Indexed Cost of Acquisition = ₹30 lakh × (348/711) = ₹14.68 lakh**

Now, the **LTCG = ₹60 lakh – ₹14.68 lakh = ₹45.32 lakh**
The taxable LTCG would then be taxed at 20% with indexation.

8.4 Exemptions on Capital Gains

To encourage reinvestment, the Income Tax Act provides several exemptions that allow you to avoid paying taxes on capital gains if you reinvest the profits in specific assets. Here are the most common exemptions:

Section 54: Reinvestment in a New House Property

If you sell a **residential property** and reinvest the proceeds in buying or constructing a new residential property, you can claim an exemption on the capital gains under **Section 54**. Key conditions include:

- The new property must be purchased within **2 years** of the sale or constructed within **3 years**.
- The exemption is limited to the cost of the new property. If your capital gains exceed the cost of the new property, the excess amount is taxable.

Section 54EC: Investment in Bonds

If you don't want to reinvest in property, you can invest the capital gains in **specified bonds** (like those issued by the **National Highway Authority of India (NHAI)** or **Rural Electrification Corporation (REC)**) to claim an exemption under **Section 54EC**.

- You must invest in these bonds within **6 months** of selling the asset.
- The maximum exemption available is ₹50 lakh.
- The bonds have a lock-in period of **5 years**.

Section 54F: Reinvestment in Residential Property (for Other Assets)

If you sell a capital asset (other than a house property) like shares, mutual funds, or land, and reinvest the proceeds in a new residential property, you can claim an exemption under **Section 54F**.

- The entire sale consideration must be reinvested, not just the capital gains, to get full exemption.

- If only part of the sale consideration is reinvested, a proportionate exemption is allowed.

8.5 Capital Losses: Offsetting Gains

Not all investments lead to profits. Sometimes, you might sell an asset at a loss. The tax system allows you to use **capital losses** to offset your **capital gains**, which helps reduce your overall tax liability.

Set-Off Rules

- **Short-Term Capital Losses (STCL)**: These can be set off against both **short-term** and **long-term capital gains**.
- **Long-Term Capital Losses (LTCL)**: These can only be set off against **long-term capital gains**.

For example, if you have a short-term capital loss of ₹50,000 from the sale of shares and a long-term capital gain of ₹1 lakh from the sale of a property, you can set off the ₹50,000 loss against the gain, reducing your taxable capital gain to ₹50,000.

Carry Forward of Losses

If you are unable to set off all your capital losses in the same financial year, you can **carry forward the losses** for up to **8 years**, provided you file your income tax return on time.

Capital gains tax can take a significant chunk out of your profits, but with careful planning, you can reduce your tax burden. Here are a few tax-saving tips:

1. Hold Investments for the Long Term

Since long-term capital gains are taxed at lower rates than short-term gains (especially for equity shares and mutual funds), holding investments for the long term can result in significant tax savings.

2. Use Indexation Benefits for Property

When selling real estate or other assets held for more than 2 years, take advantage of indexation to reduce the taxable gain. Indexation allows you to factor in inflation, reducing the capital gains subject to tax.

3. Reinvest in Exempt Assets

To avoid paying taxes on large capital gains, consider reinvesting in another house property or specified bonds under **Sections 54, 54F, or 54EC**.

4. Offset Gains with Losses

Make sure to use any capital losses to offset your gains, reducing your overall taxable amount. Plan your investments in such a way that you can strategically use losses to minimize tax on gains.

Conclusion

Capital gains are an important part of managing your investments and taxes, and knowing how to calculate them can help you save significantly. Whether you're selling shares, mutual funds, or property, understanding the tax implications and available exemptions will ensure you retain more of your profits. By planning ahead and using the exemptions allowed under the Income Tax Act, you can lower your tax liability and maximize your investment returns.

In the next chapter, we'll discuss **Income from Other Sources**, covering how interest, dividends, and other miscellaneous incomes are taxed.

Income from Other Sources

Interest, Dividends, and Gifts: Taxing the Extra Income

9.1 Introduction to Income from Other Sources

Sometimes, you earn money from sources that don't fit into the typical categories like salary, house property, or business. These earnings, which could be from bank interest, dividends, gifts, or even winnings from lotteries, are taxed under the category of **Income from Other Sources**. This head acts as a catch-all for any income that isn't taxed under the other specific heads.

In this chapter, we'll explore what constitutes **Income from Other Sources**, how it's taxed, and the available deductions that can help you reduce your tax liability.

9.2 What Qualifies as Income from Other Sources?

Here are some of the most common types of income that are taxed under **Income from Other Sources**:

Interest Income

- **Interest from Savings Accounts**: Any interest you earn from a savings bank account is taxable. However, you can claim a deduction of up to ₹10,000 per annum under **Section 80TTA**.

- **Interest from Fixed Deposits (FDs)**: Interest earned from fixed deposits in banks or post offices is fully taxable. There are no specific exemptions for FD interest, and banks may deduct **Tax Deducted at Source (TDS)** if the interest earned exceeds ₹40,000 in a financial year.
- **Interest from Bonds**: If you earn interest from bonds, it's also taxable under this head, with no special exemptions.

Dividend Income

- Dividends earned from shares or mutual funds were previously exempt, but as of FY 2020-21, dividends are fully taxable at your slab rate. Companies deduct **TDS at 10%** on dividends if the total dividend paid exceeds ₹5,000.

Income from Gifts

- **Gifts from Relatives**: Gifts received from specified relatives (like parents, siblings, or spouse) are exempt from tax, no matter the amount.
- **Gifts from Non-Relatives**: If you receive gifts worth more than ₹50,000 from non-relatives in a financial year, the entire amount is taxable as income.

- **Wedding Gifts**: Any gifts received on the occasion of your wedding, irrespective of their value or source, are exempt from tax.
- **Gifts on Special Occasions**: Gifts received under inheritance or through a will are also tax-free, but gifts received on other occasions, like birthdays or anniversaries, from non-relatives are taxable if they exceed ₹50,000.

Winnings from Lotteries, Gambling, and Game Shows

- Any income from lotteries, horse racing, gambling, game shows (such as KBC or other quiz competitions), and card games is fully taxable at a flat rate of **30%**, without allowing any deductions.

Income from Rent on Sub-Letting

- If you have sub-let a house or property you're renting, the rent you receive is taxed under **Income from Other Sources**, even though the property itself is owned by someone else.

Family Pension

- If you receive a pension from a deceased family member, this is taxable under **Income from Other Sources**. However, you can claim a deduction of **₹15,000 or 1/3rd of the pension**, whichever is lower.

- **Interest from Provident Fund (PF) Contributions**: If your employer's contribution to your Provident Fund exceeds ₹2.5 lakh annually, the interest earned on the excess is taxable under **Income from Other Sources**.
- **Rental income from machinery, plant, or furniture**: If you rent out machinery, plants, or furniture (without transferring ownership), the rental income is taxable under this head.

9.3 How to Calculate Income from Other Sources

Calculating **Income from Other Sources** is relatively simple:

- **Income = Total Receipts – Any Allowable Deductions** (where applicable).

Let's take a look at how this applies to common income streams.

Interest Income Example

If you earned ₹40,000 as interest from your fixed deposits in a bank and ₹12,000 as interest from your savings account, your taxable income would be:

- **FD Interest**: ₹40,000 (fully taxable).

- **Savings Account Interest**: ₹12,000, but you can claim a deduction of ₹10,000 under Section 80TTA, leaving ₹2,000 as taxable.

Total Taxable Income from Interest = ₹40,000 + ₹2,000 = ₹42,000.

Dividend Income Example

If you earned ₹50,000 in dividends from shares, the entire amount would be taxable under **Income from Other Sources** at your applicable income tax slab rate.

Gift Income Example

If you received a cash gift of ₹1 lakh from a friend, the amount over ₹50,000 (i.e., ₹50,000) would be considered taxable income.

9.4 Deductions for Income from Other Sources

While **Income from Other Sources** is typically fully taxable, there are a few specific deductions you can claim to reduce your tax burden.

Deduction of Expenses for Earning Income

If you've incurred any expenses to earn income that falls under this head, you can claim those expenses as deductions. For example:

- **Commission or Fees**: If you had to pay a commission to earn interest or dividends, you can deduct this expense from your total income.

- **Repairs and Insurance for Plant or Machinery**: If you rent out any machinery or furniture, the cost of repairs and insurance premiums can be deducted.

Interest on Loan for Investments

If you've taken out a loan to invest in assets that generate taxable income (such as fixed deposits or bonds), the interest paid on this loan can be claimed as a deduction.

80TTA for Savings Account Interest

You can claim a deduction of up to ₹10,000 on interest earned from a savings bank account under **Section 80TTA**. However, this deduction does not apply to interest earned from fixed deposits, recurring deposits, or corporate bonds.

Section 80TTB for Senior Citizens

For senior citizens, the **80TTB deduction** allows them to claim a deduction of up to ₹50,000 on interest earned from savings accounts, fixed deposits, or post office deposits.

9.5 Tax Rates for Income from Other Sources

The tax rates for most types of income under this head depend on your **income tax slab**. However, certain types of income are taxed at flat rates:

- **Winnings from lotteries, gambling, or game shows**: Flat **30%** tax rate.
- **Gifts from non-relatives exceeding ₹50,000**: Taxable at your slab rate.
- **Interest, dividends, and other miscellaneous income**: Taxable at your slab rate.

9.6 Tax Planning for Income from Other Sources

While most income under this head is fully taxable, smart tax planning can help you reduce your overall liability. Here are a few tips:

1. Maximize Savings Account Interest Deduction (80TTA/80TTB)

If you are earning interest from savings accounts, make sure to claim the deduction available under **Section 80TTA** (up to ₹10,000) or **80TTB** (up to ₹50,000 for senior citizens). This simple step can significantly reduce your taxable income.

2. Structure Gifts Carefully

If you expect to receive a large gift, try to structure it in a way that ensures it comes from a **relative**, or as a **wedding gift**, both of which are tax-exempt. Gifts received as part of inheritance are also tax-free.

3. Declare Dividend Income

As dividends are now fully taxable, ensure that you declare them while filing your income tax returns.

TDS is deducted by companies on dividends exceeding ₹5,000, but if your income is below the taxable threshold, you can claim a refund for the TDS deducted.

Conclusion

Income from Other Sources may not be your primary income, but it still plays an important role in your overall tax liability. By understanding how interest, dividends, gifts, and other miscellaneous income are taxed, and by using available deductions, you can minimize your tax burden effectively.

In the next chapter, we'll explore **Tax Rebates** and learn how taxpayers with lower incomes can benefit from special tax rebates to reduce their total tax liability.

Tax Rebates

Reduce Your Tax Bill with Special Rebates Under Section 87A

10.1 Introduction to Tax Rebates

Tax rebates offer direct relief by reducing your overall tax liability after you've computed your income and applied deductions. One of the most significant rebates available to individual taxpayers in India is under **Section 87A**, which benefits those with lower income by reducing their tax payable. Rebates work differently from **deductions** or **exemptions**—while deductions reduce taxable income, rebates directly reduce the tax payable.

In this chapter, we'll focus on the **Section 87A rebate**, its eligibility, and how it can help reduce your tax bill to zero if you meet certain criteria.

10.2 What is a Tax Rebate?

A **tax rebate** is an amount that is directly subtracted from your total tax payable. Unlike deductions or exemptions, which reduce your taxable income, a rebate reduces the actual amount of tax you owe after calculating your total tax liability. For instance, if your total tax payable is ₹10,000 and you qualify for a rebate of ₹5,000, you'll only need to pay ₹5,000 in taxes.

Section 87A provides a rebate on tax for individuals whose total income does not exceed a specified limit. It's a provision aimed at reducing the tax burden for low-income earners.

Eligibility for Section 87A

To claim the rebate under **Section 87A**, you need to meet the following criteria:

1. **Residential Status**: You must be a resident individual (both senior and non-senior citizens can avail this rebate). Non-resident individuals (NRIs) are not eligible for the rebate.
2. **Total Income**: Your total taxable income (after deductions) must be **₹5 lakh or less** in a financial year.

Amount of Rebate

The maximum rebate you can claim under **Section 87A** is **₹12,500**. This means:

- If your calculated tax payable is **₹12,500 or less**, you won't have to pay any tax.
- If your calculated tax payable is more than **₹12,500**, the rebate will be restricted to ₹12,500.

Impact of Section 87A

If your total taxable income is **₹5 lakh or less**, this rebate can completely eliminate your tax liability, meaning you won't have to pay any tax at all. However, if your income exceeds ₹5 lakh after applying deductions, you won't be eligible for the rebate.

10.4 How Section 87A Rebate Works: An Example

Let's break down an example to see how Section 87A works in practice:

Example 1: Income Less than ₹5 Lakh (Eligible for Rebate)
Rahul's total taxable income after deductions is ₹4.8 lakh. Based on the current tax slabs, his tax liability is calculated as follows:

- Income up to ₹2.5 lakh: **No tax**.
- Income between ₹2.5 lakh and ₹5 lakh: **5% tax on ₹2.3 lakh = ₹11,500**.

Tax payable before rebate = ₹11,500.
Since his income is less than ₹5 lakh, Rahul is eligible for the **Section 87A rebate**. His total tax payable after the rebate will be:

- ₹11,500 (tax) – ₹11,500 (rebate) = ₹0.

In this case, Rahul won't have to pay any tax.

INCOME TAX FOR THE LAYMAN

Example 2: Income More than ₹5 Lakh (Not Eligible for Rebate)

Sneha's total taxable income after deductions is ₹5.2 lakh. Based on the current tax slabs, her tax liability is calculated as follows:

- Income up to ₹2.5 lakh: **No tax**.
- Income between ₹2.5 lakh and ₹5 lakh: **5% tax on ₹2.5 lakh = ₹12,500**.
- Income above ₹5 lakh: **10% tax on ₹20,000 = ₹2,000**.

Tax payable before rebate = ₹14,500.
Since Sneha's income exceeds ₹5 lakh, she is **not eligible** for the Section 87A rebate. Hence, she will have to pay the full **₹14,500** in taxes.

10.5 Importance of Section 87A for Low-Income Earners

Section 87A has made it possible for individuals with lower incomes to reduce their tax liability to zero, easing the financial burden. It ensures that taxpayers with a total income of up to ₹5 lakh won't have to pay any taxes at all. For many, this provision serves as a significant relief, especially those earning close to the ₹5 lakh limit.

10.6 How to Claim the Section 87A Rebate

Claiming the Section 87A rebate is a straightforward process. Here's how it works:

1. **Calculate Your Total Taxable Income:** Add up all your sources of income, including

salary, interest, rental income, or business income, and subtract any deductions you're eligible for, like under **Section 80C** or **80D**.

2. **Compute Your Tax Liability**: Apply the income tax slabs to calculate the total tax due based on your taxable income.

3. **Apply the Rebate**: If your total taxable income is ₹5 lakh or less, apply the **Section 87A rebate** to reduce your tax payable by up to ₹12,500.

4. **Final Tax Liability**: If the rebate reduces your tax liability to zero, you won't have to pay any tax. Otherwise, you'll need to pay the remaining amount after applying the rebate.

10.7 Other Important Rebates

While Section 87A is the most common rebate for individual taxpayers, there are other rebates and reliefs available in specific situations. Here are some additional rebate provisions that could benefit you:

1. Rebate for Agricultural Income

If a portion of your income comes from agricultural activities, it may qualify for exemption. Agricultural income is exempt from tax, but it may affect the rate at which your other income is taxed, known as **partial integration**.

2. Rebate for Arrears of Salary (Section 89)

If you receive salary arrears or a pension in a lump sum that relates to previous financial years, you may be eligible for a rebate under **Section 89**. This rebate prevents you from paying a higher tax rate due to income from earlier years being taxed in the current year.

10.8 Section 87A in the Context of the New vs. Old Tax Regime

With the introduction of the **new tax regime**, which offers lower tax rates but no deductions or exemptions, it's essential to know that the **Section 87A rebate** is available under both the old and new regimes.

Old Tax Regime:

- Under the old regime, you can claim deductions under **Section 80C, 80D**, and others, which help reduce your total taxable income to ₹5 lakh or below to claim the rebate.

New Tax Regime:

- Under the new tax regime, the **Section 87A rebate** is also available if your total taxable income is below ₹5 lakh. However, you won't be able to claim deductions like **Section 80C** or **80D**, so you'll need to be mindful of your income before opting for this regime.

10.9 Key Takeaways for Maximizing the Section 87A Rebate

Here are a few practical tips to ensure you make the most of the Section 87A rebate:

- **Plan Your Deductions**: If your income exceeds ₹5 lakh, use deductions under **Section 80C, 80D,** and other sections to reduce your taxable income to ₹5 lakh or below. This will allow you to claim the Section 87A rebate and eliminate your tax liability.
- **Review the New vs. Old Regime**: If you're considering the new tax regime, ensure that your total income doesn't exceed ₹5 lakh after deductions to claim the Section 87A rebate.
- **Claim Arrear Rebates**: If you've received arrears or a lump sum payment, explore rebates under **Section 89** to lower your tax burden.

Conclusion

Tax rebates, especially under **Section 87A**, provide a crucial opportunity for taxpayers with lower incomes to reduce or eliminate their tax liability. By understanding how the rebate works and ensuring your income stays within the eligibility threshold, you can significantly reduce your tax burden. For those earning up to ₹5 lakh, the rebate can make a big difference, helping them retain more of their income.

INCOME TAX FOR THE LAYMAN

In the next chapter, we'll look at **Tax Benefits for Senior Citizens**, exploring special provisions, higher exemption limits, and deductions available for older taxpayers.

Tax Benefits for Senior Citizens

Special Perks for Seniors: Pay Less, Save More

11.1 Introduction to Tax Benefits for Senior Citizens

In recognition of the financial needs of senior citizens, the Indian Income Tax Act provides various **special tax benefits** to help reduce their tax burden. These benefits include higher exemption limits, additional deductions, and relaxed rules around filing returns and paying taxes.

In this chapter, we'll look at how senior citizens—defined as individuals aged **60 years or above**—can take advantage of these provisions to save more on taxes. We'll also cover the special provisions for **super senior citizens**, defined as individuals aged **80 years or above**.

11.2 Who Qualifies as a Senior Citizen?

Before exploring the specific benefits, it's important to understand how the Income Tax Act classifies senior citizens:

- **Senior Citizens**: Individuals aged **60 years or above** but less than **80 years** at any time during the financial year.
- **Super Senior Citizens**: Individuals aged **80 years or above** at any time during the financial year.

Different tax rules apply to these two categories, with **super senior citizens** receiving even higher tax benefits.

11.3 Higher Exemption Limits for Senior Citizens

One of the most significant advantages for senior citizens is the higher **basic exemption limit** compared to non-senior taxpayers.

1. Exemption for Senior Citizens (60 years and above)

- The basic exemption limit for senior citizens is ₹**3 lakh**, compared to ₹2.5 lakh for non-seniors. This means that if a senior citizen's total income is ₹3 lakh or below, no tax is payable.

2. Exemption for Super Senior Citizens (80 years and above)

- For super senior citizens, the basic exemption limit is even higher at ₹**5 lakh**. This means super seniors with income up to ₹5 lakh won't have to pay any taxes.

Example:

- If a **senior citizen** earns ₹3 lakh in a financial year, they will not have to pay any taxes.
- If a **super senior citizen** earns up to ₹5 lakh, they also won't have to pay any taxes.

This exemption limit can also be combined with deductions to further reduce taxable income for those with higher earnings.

11.4 No Advance Tax for Senior Citizens with No Business Income

Ordinarily, individuals with tax liability exceeding ₹10,000 in a financial year must pay **advance tax**. However, senior citizens who don't have income from a business or profession are **exempt from paying advance tax**. They can pay their entire tax liability at the time of filing their income tax return, easing the burden of quarterly advance tax payments.

This provision provides significant relief, especially for retirees whose primary income may come from pension, fixed deposits, or other passive income sources.

11.5 Higher Deductions Under Section 80D for Health Insurance

Health expenses tend to increase with age, and recognizing this, the Income Tax Act provides higher deductions for senior citizens under **Section 80D**.

For Senior Citizens (60 years and above)

- Senior citizens can claim a deduction of **up to ₹50,000** per financial year for **health insurance premiums** paid for themselves or their spouse.
- If a senior citizen is paying for both their own health insurance and that of their senior citizen parents, they can claim an additional deduction of **₹50,000**.

For Super Senior Citizens (80 years and above)

- If super senior citizens are **not covered by any health insurance policy**, they can claim a deduction of up to **₹50,000** on medical expenses incurred during the financial year, even without insurance.

This higher deduction limit ensures that older individuals can manage their medical costs more efficiently, reducing their taxable income by claiming these expenses.

11.6 Additional Deductions for Medical Expenses Under Section 80DDB

Section 80DDB allows for deductions on expenses incurred for the treatment of certain specified diseases for both senior and super senior citizens.

- For **senior citizens**, the maximum deduction allowed is ₹1 **lakh**.
- The list of diseases includes serious conditions like cancer, neurological diseases, chronic kidney failure, and others. To claim this deduction, the disease must be certified by a specialist doctor working in a government hospital.

This provision helps senior citizens manage significant medical expenses without a heavy tax burden.

11.7 Exemption of Interest Income for Senior Citizens (Section 80TTB)

Senior citizens can claim an exemption on the **interest income** earned from savings accounts, fixed deposits, recurring deposits, and post office deposits under **Section 80TTB**.

Key Features of Section 80TTB

- Senior citizens can claim a deduction of up to **₹50,000** on interest income.

- This applies to interest from savings accounts, fixed deposits (FDs), recurring deposits (RDs), and post office schemes.

Example:
If a senior citizen earns ₹60,000 in interest income from fixed deposits, they can claim a deduction of ₹50,000 under **Section 80TTB**, leaving only ₹10,000 as taxable income.

This is especially useful for retirees who rely on interest income for their living expenses. It's important to note that the **80TTB deduction** is available **only to senior citizens**, and it replaces the ₹10,000 deduction available to non-seniors under Section 80TTA.

11.8 Benefits for Senior Citizens on Filing ITR

For senior citizens, the process of filing income tax returns is relatively simple:

- Senior citizens earning income from salary, pension, or interest can file their ITR using the simplified **ITR-1** form, provided their income is below ₹50 lakh.
- Those who are not required to file returns online can submit their **paper returns**. This is especially helpful for senior citizens who are not familiar with digital platforms.

11.9 Tax-Free Reverse Mortgage Scheme

The **reverse mortgage** scheme is designed to help senior citizens who own a home but need a regular income stream in retirement. Under this scheme:

- Senior citizens can **mortgage their home** to a bank or financial institution and, in return, receive regular payments.
- The amount received from a reverse mortgage is **not considered taxable income**. This means that senior citizens can continue living in their own home while receiving a steady income, without any tax liability on the amount received.

11.10 Special Provisions for Super Senior Citizens

As mentioned earlier, **super senior citizens** (aged 80 years or more) enjoy even higher benefits under the Income Tax Act:

1. **Higher Exemption Limit**: ₹5 lakh basic exemption limit.
2. **Simplified Tax Filing**: Super senior citizens can file paper returns if they choose to, making the process easier for those less familiar with online filing.
3. **Medical Deductions**: Enhanced medical deductions are available, as discussed earlier, making it easier for super senior citizens to claim tax benefits on higher healthcare expenses.

11.11 Key Takeaways for Senior Citizens

Here are a few practical tax-saving tips for senior citizens:

- **Maximize Your Deductions**: Claim the higher limits available under **Section 80D** for health insurance premiums and medical expenses. Ensure that you also claim the **Section 80TTB** deduction for interest income, which is available only to senior citizens.
- **Plan Around Exemption Limits**: For **super senior citizens**, aim to keep your income below ₹5 lakh to avoid paying any tax at all. You can combine the basic exemption limit with deductions to further reduce your tax liability.
- **Take Advantage of Paper Filing**: If you're uncomfortable with e-filing, remember that both senior and super senior citizens can file paper returns.

Conclusion

Senior citizens in India are offered several tax benefits to ease their financial burden. From higher exemption limits to deductions on health insurance and interest income, these provisions help reduce their overall tax liability. By taking advantage of these benefits, senior citizens can retain more of their income and enjoy a secure financial future during their retirement years.

In the next chapter, we'll explore how to choose between the **Old and New Tax Regime**, offering insights on which option might be more beneficial depending on your income and deductions.

Choosing Between Old and New Tax Regime

Old vs. New: Which Tax Regime is Right?

12.1 Introduction to the Two Tax Regimes

In the Union Budget of 2020, the government introduced a new optional **tax regime** with lower tax rates but no deductions or exemptions. This created a choice for taxpayers: stick with the **old regime** with its deductions and exemptions, or switch to the **new regime** for potentially lower tax rates but fewer benefits.

Choosing between the old and new tax regime isn't always straightforward. The decision depends on your income level, the deductions you claim, and your financial situation. In this chapter, we'll explore the key differences between the two regimes, how they apply to different taxpayers, and offer guidance on making the right choice for your specific circumstances.

12.2 Understanding the Old Tax Regime

The **old tax regime** operates with higher tax rates but allows taxpayers to claim a wide variety of deductions and exemptions. These include:

- **Deductions under Section 80C, 80D, 80E**, etc.

- Exemptions such as **House Rent Allowance (HRA), Leave Travel Allowance (LTA),** and **Standard Deduction.**

Under the old regime, you can lower your taxable income by claiming deductions on investments like **Public Provident Fund (PPF), Employee Provident Fund (EPF),** insurance premiums, and home loan repayments.

Old Regime Tax Slabs (FY 2023-24):

- Income up to ₹2.5 lakh: **No tax.**
- Income between **₹2.5 lakh and ₹5 lakh: 5%.**
- Income between **₹5 lakh and ₹10 lakh: 20%.**
- Income above ₹10 lakh: **30%.**

Key Features of the Old Regime:

- Allows for multiple **deductions and exemptions,** reducing taxable income.
- Higher **tax rates,** especially for those in higher income brackets.
- More beneficial for taxpayers who invest heavily in tax-saving instruments or have significant exemptions like **HRA.**

12.3 Understanding the New Tax Regime

The **new tax regime** offers **lower tax rates** but removes most deductions and exemptions. This regime simplifies the tax filing process but is less beneficial for individuals who depend on deductions to lower their taxable income.

New Regime Tax Slabs (FY 2023-24):

- Income up to ₹2.5 lakh: **No tax**.
- Income between ₹2.5 lakh and ₹5 lakh: **5%**.
- Income between ₹5 lakh and ₹7.5 lakh: **10%**.
- Income between ₹7.5 lakh and ₹10 lakh: **15%**.
- Income between ₹10 lakh and ₹12.5 lakh: **20%**.
- Income between ₹12.5 lakh and ₹15 lakh: **25%**.
- Income above ₹15 lakh: **30%**.

Key Features of the New Regime:

- Lower tax rates compared to the old regime.
- No deductions or exemptions (e.g., no 80C, 80D, HRA, or Standard Deduction).
- Beneficial for taxpayers with limited investments in tax-saving instruments.

12.4 Key Differences Between the Old and New Tax Regimes

To decide between the old and new regime, it's important to understand the key differences:

Feature	Old Regime	New Regime
Tax Rates	Higher tax rates	Lower tax rates
Deductions under Section 80C	Allowed (up to ₹1.5 lakh)	Not allowed
Deductions under Section 80D	Allowed (for health insurance premiums)	Not allowed
House Rent Allowance (HRA)	Allowed	Not allowed
Leave Travel Allowance (LTA)	Allowed	Not allowed
Standard Deduction	Allowed (₹50,000)	Not allowed
Simplicity	Requires more calculations	Simpler, with fewer calculations
Best for	Taxpayers with many deductions	Taxpayers without

Feature	Old Regime	New Regime
		significant deductions

12.5 When Should You Choose the Old Regime?

The old tax regime is typically better for taxpayers who:

1. **Maximize Deductions**: If you heavily invest in tax-saving instruments (like **PPF, ELSS, life insurance**, or **EPF**) or have other deductions like **home loan interest**, the old regime may reduce your tax liability significantly.
2. **Claim Exemptions**: If you receive **HRA** and claim other exemptions like **LTA**, the old regime allows you to take advantage of these.
3. **Medical and Insurance Deductions**: If you're paying high premiums for health insurance or have significant medical expenses, deductions under **Section 80D** and other sections will help reduce your taxable income in the old regime.

Example:

Priya's income is ₹9 lakh annually, and she invests ₹1.5 lakh in **PPF** under **Section 80C**. She also pays

₹25,000 in **health insurance premiums** (eligible for deduction under **Section 80D**).
Under the **old regime**, Priya can claim deductions totaling ₹1.75 lakh, reducing her taxable income to **₹7.25 lakh**. Her tax liability would be:

- ₹2.5 lakh: **No tax.**
- ₹2.5 lakh to ₹5 lakh: **5% = ₹12,500.**
- ₹5 lakh to ₹7.25 lakh: **20% = ₹45,000.**
  Total tax payable = ₹57,500.

12.6 When Should You Choose the New Regime?

The new tax regime is beneficial for individuals who:

1. **Don't Have Many Deductions**: If you don't claim many deductions or exemptions, the lower tax rates of the new regime might result in a lower tax liability.
2. **Want Simplicity**: With no need to calculate exemptions and deductions, the new regime is simpler and faster to file.

Example:

Ravi earns ₹9 lakh annually but doesn't invest in **PPF** or claim any significant deductions. Under the **new regime**, his taxable income remains at ₹9 lakh, and his tax liability would be:

- ₹2.5 lakh: **No tax.**
- ₹2.5 lakh to ₹5 lakh: **5% = ₹12,500.**
- ₹5 lakh to ₹7.5 lakh: **10% = ₹25,000.**

- ₹7.5 lakh to ₹9 lakh: **15% = ₹22,500.
  Total tax payable = ₹60,000**.

In this case, Ravi's total tax in the new regime is slightly higher than Priya's tax under the old regime, but since he doesn't have significant deductions to claim, the new regime is simpler for him.

12.7 Evaluating the Regimes: A Practical Approach

To determine which regime is right for you, follow these steps:

1. **List Your Deductions and Exemptions**: Add up all the deductions you're eligible for under the old regime, such as **Section 80C, HRA, Standard Deduction**, and others.
2. **Calculate Your Tax Under the Old Regime**: Subtract the total deductions from your gross income and calculate the tax liability using the old regime's slabs.
3. **Calculate Your Tax Under the New Regime**: Without applying any deductions, calculate your tax based on the lower rates of the new regime.
4. **Compare**: Compare the tax liabilities under both regimes. The regime with the lower tax liability will likely be the best choice for you.

12.8 Which Regime is Better for You?

There is no one-size-fits-all answer when choosing between the old and new tax regimes. Here's a general guideline:

- **If you have significant deductions** (like investments, health insurance, HRA), the **old regime** will likely be more beneficial.
- **If you don't claim many deductions**, or prefer simplicity, the **new regime** may be better, especially if your income is moderate (₹7-12 lakh).

12.9 Flexibility in Switching Between Regimes

One important benefit of the new regime is that **salaried individuals** can switch between the old and new regimes every financial year. However, if you have **business income**, you are allowed to switch regimes only once.

This flexibility allows you to reassess your financial situation each year and choose the most beneficial regime based on your income, expenses, and tax-saving strategies.

Conclusion

Choosing between the old and new tax regime is a personal decision that depends on your income, investments, and financial goals. The old regime, with its deductions and exemptions, is better for individuals with significant tax-saving investments, while the new regime.

Deductions and Exemptions You Can Claim

Claim What's Yours: Reduce Your Tax Bill Legally

13.1 Introduction to Deductions and Exemptions

Deductions and exemptions are essential tools for reducing your taxable income, ultimately lowering your overall tax liability. The **Income Tax Act** provides a wide range of deductions and exemptions that individuals can claim to reduce their tax burden legally. These provisions encourage taxpayers to save, invest, and plan for their future.

In this chapter, we'll cover the most common deductions and exemptions, how they work, and how to maximize their benefits to lower your tax liability.

13.2 The Difference Between Deductions and Exemptions

Before diving into the specific sections, it's important to understand the distinction between **deductions** and **exemptions**:

- **Deductions** reduce your **taxable income** after it has been computed. For example, deductions under **Section 80C** allow you to reduce your taxable income by investing in specific instruments like **PPF** or **life insurance**.

- **Exemptions** reduce your income **before it is added to your total taxable income**. For example, **House Rent Allowance (HRA)** and **Leave Travel Allowance (LTA)** are exemptions that directly reduce your salary income.

13.3 Section 80C: The Most Popular Deduction

Section 80C is the most widely used section for tax-saving investments, offering a maximum deduction of **₹1.5 lakh**. You can claim this deduction by investing in various instruments, which are often long-term savings options.

Common Investments Eligible Under 80C:

- **Public Provident Fund (PPF)**: A popular long-term savings scheme with a lock-in period of 15 years. The contributions you make are eligible for a deduction under **80C**, and the interest earned is tax-free.
- **Employees' Provident Fund (EPF)**: Mandatory for salaried employees, contributions to **EPF** are eligible for a deduction under 80C.
- **Life Insurance Premiums**: Premiums paid for life insurance policies for yourself, your spouse, or your children are eligible for deduction under **80C**.
- **Equity-Linked Savings Scheme (ELSS)**: ELSS mutual funds are tax-saving investment options that have a lock-in period of 3 years.

The returns are market-linked, and you can claim the investment amount as a deduction under **80C**.

- **National Savings Certificate (NSC)**: A government-backed savings instrument, NSC offers fixed returns with a lock-in period of 5 years. Contributions are eligible for deduction under **80C**.
- **Home Loan Principal Repayment**: The **principal repayment** on your home loan qualifies for a deduction under **Section 80C**.
- **Children's Tuition Fees**: The tuition fees paid for your children's education are also eligible for deduction under **80C**.

Maximum Deduction: You can claim a maximum deduction of ₹1.5 lakh under Section 80C, regardless of how many investments you make in the eligible instruments.

13.4 Section 80D: Health Insurance Premiums

Section 80D allows taxpayers to claim a deduction for **health insurance premiums** paid for themselves, their spouse, children, and parents.

Deduction Limits Under 80D:

- **₹25,000** for health insurance premiums for yourself, spouse, and dependent children.
- **₹50,000** if the insured person (self or spouse) is a senior citizen (aged 60 or above).

- An additional **₹50,000** for premiums paid for health insurance coverage of parents (if parents are senior citizens).

Medical Expenses for Senior Citizens:

If you or your parents are senior citizens and are not covered by health insurance, you can claim a deduction of up to ₹50,000 on actual medical expenses under **Section 80D**.

Example:
Raj, aged 40, pays ₹20,000 as a health insurance premium for himself and ₹40,000 for his senior citizen parents. He can claim a deduction of ₹60,000 (₹20,000 for himself + ₹40,000 for his parents) under **Section 80D**.

13.5 Section 80E: Interest on Education Loans

Section 80E allows a deduction for the **interest paid on education loans**. This is especially useful for individuals who have taken out loans for higher education.

Key Features:

- The deduction applies only to the **interest component** of the loan, not the principal.
- There is **no maximum limit** on the amount of interest you can claim as a deduction.

- The deduction can be claimed for **up to 8 years** starting from the year in which the repayment begins, or until the interest is paid in full, whichever is earlier.

Example:
If Amit is paying ₹50,000 annually as interest on his education loan, he can claim this entire amount as a deduction under **Section 80E**, reducing his taxable income accordingly.

13.6 Section 80TTA and 80TTB: Interest on Savings Accounts and Fixed Deposits

Section 80TTA provides a deduction on **interest earned from savings accounts** with banks, post offices, or co-operative banks.

- You can claim a deduction of up to **₹10,000** on interest income from savings accounts.
- **This does not apply to fixed deposits or recurring deposits.**

Section 80TTB for Senior Citizens:

Senior citizens can claim a higher deduction under **Section 80TTB**. This allows a deduction of up to **₹50,000** on interest earned from:

- Savings accounts
- Fixed deposits (FDs)
- Recurring deposits (RDs)
- Post office schemes

Example:

If Mrs. Sharma, a senior citizen, earns ₹60,000 as interest from her fixed deposit, she can claim a deduction of ₹50,000 under **Section 80TTB**, leaving only ₹10,000 as taxable income.

13.7 Section 24: Home Loan Interest Deduction

For homeowners, **Section 24** provides a deduction on **home loan interest payments**.

- For a **self-occupied property**, you can claim a deduction of up to **₹2 lakh** on the interest paid during the financial year.
- For a **rented property**, there is **no limit** on the deduction for interest payments.

Pre-Construction Interest:

You can also claim a deduction for the interest paid during the construction phase of your house. The interest paid before the construction is completed can be claimed in **five equal installments** starting from the year the construction is completed.

Example:

If Nisha is paying ₹3 lakh annually as home loan interest for a self-occupied property, she can claim a maximum deduction of ₹2 lakh under **Section 24**, and the remaining ₹1 lakh will not be deductible.

13.8 Section 80G: Donations to Charitable Institutions

If you donate to eligible charitable institutions or relief funds, you can claim a deduction under **Section 80G**. Donations can be made to:

- National relief funds (like the **PM Relief Fund** or **PM CARES Fund**).
- Approved charitable organizations and non-profits.

Key Features:

- Donations are eligible for **50% or 100%** deduction, depending on the organization.
- In some cases, there is a **cap** on the deduction amount (limited to **10% of your gross total income**), but donations to specific funds like the **PM CARES Fund** are eligible for a full deduction with no cap.

13.9 Other Notable Deductions and Exemptions

Here are a few additional deductions and exemptions you can claim:

1. Section 80GGC: Donations to Political Parties

You can claim a deduction for contributions made to **political parties** under **Section 80GGC**. There is no upper limit on the amount that can be deducted.

2. Section 80CCD: National Pension Scheme (NPS)

Contributions to the **National Pension Scheme (NPS)** can help you claim an additional deduction of ₹50,000 under **Section 80CCD(1B)**, over and above the ₹1.5 lakh allowed under Section 80C.

3. House Rent Allowance (HRA)

If you live in rented accommodation, you can claim an **HRA exemption**. The exemption amount depends on:

- Your salary.
- The rent paid.
- Whether you live in a metro or non-metro city.

4. Leave Travel Allowance (LTA)

If your employer provides an **LTA** benefit, you can claim an exemption for travel expenses incurred while on leave. This can only be claimed for domestic travel and does not cover accommodation or other expenses.

Conclusion

By making the most of the deductions and exemptions available under the Income Tax Act, you can significantly reduce your taxable income and, in turn, lower your tax liability. Whether it's through investments, insurance premiums, home loan repayments, or charitable donations, each deduction helps you save money and encourages financial discipline.

Section 80C: The Most Popular Tax-Saving Options

Maximize Your Savings with the Power of 80C

14.1 Introduction to Section 80C

Section 80C is the most widely used section of the Income Tax Act for tax-saving purposes. It offers a deduction of up to ₹1.5 lakh on certain specified investments and expenses, allowing you to reduce your taxable income significantly. The tax benefits under Section 80C encourage individuals to save for the future while also reducing their current tax liabilities.

In this chapter, we'll explore the most popular tax-saving options under Section 80C, how they work, and how to use them effectively to maximize your tax savings.

14.2 Key Investments Eligible Under Section 80C

The primary objective of Section 80C is to promote saving and investment among taxpayers. There are a variety of investment options available under this section, each with its own benefits, returns, and lock-in periods.

Here are some of the most common and beneficial investment options under Section 80C:

1. Public Provident Fund (PPF)

PPF is one of the most popular long-term savings schemes in India due to its safety, government backing, and tax benefits.

- **Returns**: PPF offers interest at a rate set by the government (around 7-8% annually), which is entirely tax-free.
- **Lock-in Period**: The lock-in period is **15 years**, but partial withdrawals are allowed after the 7th year.
- **Tax Benefit**: Investments in PPF are eligible for a deduction of up to ₹1.5 lakh under **Section 80C**, and both the interest earned and the maturity amount are completely tax-free.

2. Employee Provident Fund (EPF)

EPF is a mandatory savings scheme for salaried employees in which both the employee and employer contribute a percentage of the employee's salary.

- **Contribution**: 12% of your basic salary is automatically deducted and contributed to your EPF account. The employer also contributes, but only the employee's contribution is eligible for deduction under **Section 80C**.
- **Tax Benefit**: You can claim a deduction on the amount you contribute to EPF under

Section 80C, and the interest earned is tax-free, provided the account is held for 5 years.

3. National Savings Certificate (NSC)

The **NSC** is a fixed-income investment offered by the post office, which guarantees a fixed return and is suitable for risk-averse investors.

- **Returns**: The interest rate for NSC is around 6-7% and is fixed by the government.
- **Lock-in Period**: The lock-in period is **5 years**.
- **Tax Benefit**: Investments in NSC are eligible for deduction under Section 80C, and the interest earned (though taxable) can also be reinvested in NSC to claim further deductions.

4. Equity-Linked Savings Scheme (ELSS)

ELSS mutual funds are market-linked tax-saving instruments with higher potential returns but come with market risks.

- **Returns**: Returns vary based on market performance, but historically, ELSS has provided returns of 10-15%.
- **Lock-in Period**: ELSS has the shortest lock-in period of **3 years** among all 80C investments.
- **Tax Benefit**: Investments in ELSS are eligible for deduction under Section 80C, and any

long-term capital gains (LTCG) over ₹1 lakh are taxed at 10%.

5. Life Insurance Premiums

Premiums paid for **life insurance policies** for yourself, your spouse, or your children are eligible for deductions under Section 80C.

- **Tax Benefit**: The deduction is available up to the ₹1.5 lakh limit, and the maturity benefits from policies (like **endowment** or **term insurance**) are usually tax-free, provided specific conditions are met.

6. Senior Citizen Savings Scheme (SCSS)

The **SCSS** is a government-backed savings scheme designed specifically for senior citizens, offering higher returns with safety.

- **Returns**: SCSS offers around **8-9% interest**, which is paid quarterly.
- **Lock-in Period**: The lock-in period is **5 years**, but the account can be extended for another 3 years.
- **Tax Benefit**: Contributions to SCSS are eligible for a deduction under **Section 80C**, but the interest earned is taxable.

14.3 Key Expenses Eligible Under Section 80C

Apart from investments, certain expenses are also eligible for deductions under Section 80C. These include:

1. Home Loan Principal Repayment

If you've taken a home loan, the **principal** component of your **home loan repayment** qualifies for deduction under **Section 80C**.

- **Eligibility**: You can claim this deduction only after the construction of the property is completed.
- **Tax Benefit**: Up to ₹1.5 lakh of the principal repayment can be claimed as a deduction under Section 80C.

2. Children's Tuition Fees

The **tuition fees** paid for your children's education (for up to two children) in recognized institutions are eligible for deduction under **Section 80C**.

- **Scope**: This includes schools, colleges, universities, and other educational institutions.
- **Tax Benefit**: You can claim up to ₹1.5 lakh as a deduction under Section 80C, but this amount is clubbed with other 80C investments.

3. Life Insurance Premiums

As mentioned earlier, premiums paid for life insurance policies (including policies for your spouse or children) are also eligible under **Section 80C**.

14.4 Maximizing Your 80C Deductions

To get the maximum benefit from Section 80C, here are a few practical tips:

1. Diversify Your Investments

While traditional investments like **PPF** and **EPF** offer safety and fixed returns, you can diversify your portfolio by investing in market-linked instruments like **ELSS**. ELSS provides the shortest lock-in period with potential for higher returns, but it carries market risk.

2. Combine Investments and Expenses

Since both investments and specific expenses are eligible under **Section 80C**, you can combine them to reach the ₹1.5 lakh limit. For example, if your **home loan principal** repayment is ₹70,000 and your **PPF** contribution is ₹80,000, you've already utilized ₹1.5 lakh of the deduction.

3. Start Early

The earlier you start investing in 80C instruments like **PPF** or **NSC**, the more you can benefit from compounded returns over the long term, while simultaneously reducing your annual tax liability.

14.5 Limitations of Section 80C

Although Section 80C offers several tax-saving opportunities, it also comes with some limitations:

- **Capped at ₹1.5 lakh**: No matter how many investments you make under 80C, the total deduction limit is capped at ₹1.5 lakh, which means you may not get a deduction for every rupee invested if you exceed this amount.
- **Long Lock-In Periods**: Most 80C investments, such as **PPF** (15 years), **NSC** (5 years), and **SCSS** (5 years), come with long lock-in periods, making them less liquid.

Conclusion

Section 80C remains the most popular and widely used section for tax-saving investments. By choosing the right mix of safe and market-linked instruments, as well as eligible expenses, you can reduce your taxable income and save significantly on taxes. However, understanding the lock-in periods and returns associated with each investment is essential for effective tax planning.

In the next chapter, we'll explore **Other Key Deductions (80D, 80E, etc.)**, focusing on deductions related to health insurance, education loans, and more, that can further reduce your tax liability.

Other Key Deductions

Beyond 80C: Additional Deductions

15.1 Introduction to Other Key Deductions

While **Section 80C** is the most commonly used deduction, the Income Tax Act provides many other sections that offer tax-saving benefits. Deductions under these sections can significantly reduce your taxable income when used alongside 80C. These include deductions for health insurance, education loans, savings account interest, and more.

In this chapter, we will explore the most important tax-saving deductions beyond Section 80C and how to use them effectively.

15.2 Section 80D: Deduction for Health Insurance Premiums

Section 80D allows taxpayers to claim a deduction for **health insurance premiums** paid for themselves, their spouse, children, and parents. It also covers medical expenses for senior citizens who are not covered by health insurance.

Deduction Limits Under 80D:

- **₹25,000** for health insurance premiums paid for yourself, spouse, and dependent children.

- **₹50,000** if the insured person (self or spouse) is a senior citizen (aged 60 or above).
- An additional **₹50,000** for health insurance premiums paid for senior citizen parents.
- If your parents are senior citizens and uninsured, you can claim a deduction of up to ₹50,000 for medical expenses.

Example:
If Ankit pays ₹25,000 for his health insurance and ₹40,000 for his senior citizen parents, he can claim a total deduction of ₹65,000 under **Section 80D**.

Preventive Health Check-Up:

A maximum of ₹5,000 can be claimed within the overall 80D limit for expenses related to preventive health check-ups.

15.3 Section 80E: Deduction for Interest on Education Loans

Section 80E allows for a deduction on the **interest paid on education loans**. This is useful for individuals who have taken loans to fund higher education for themselves or their dependents.

Key Features:

- Only the **interest component** of the loan is eligible for deduction, not the principal.

- There is **no upper limit** on the amount of interest you can claim as a deduction.
- The deduction can be claimed for **up to 8 years** from the year the loan repayment starts, or until the interest is fully paid off, whichever is earlier.
- The loan must be for pursuing higher education from recognized institutions.

Example:

If Suman is paying ₹60,000 annually as interest on her education loan, she can claim this entire amount as a deduction under **Section 80E**, reducing her taxable income by ₹60,000.

15.4 Section 80TTA: Deduction for Interest on Savings Account

Section 80TTA provides a deduction on the **interest earned from savings accounts** held in banks, post offices, or co-operative banks. This deduction is available to individuals and HUFs (Hindu Undivided Families).

Key Features:

- The maximum deduction available under 80TTA is **₹10,000**.
- This deduction applies only to interest earned from **savings accounts**. Interest from **fixed deposits (FDs)** or **recurring deposits (RDs)** is not eligible for deduction.

Example:

If Megha earns ₹12,000 as interest from her savings account, she can claim a deduction of ₹10,000 under **Section 80TTA**, and only ₹2,000 will be taxable.

15.5 Section 80TTB: Deduction for Interest on Savings for Senior Citizens

Section 80TTB is a special provision that allows senior citizens to claim a higher deduction on the interest earned from **savings accounts, fixed deposits (FDs), recurring deposits (RDs)**, and **post office schemes**.

Key Features:

- Senior citizens can claim a deduction of up to **₹50,000** on interest income.
- This applies to both interest from savings accounts and fixed deposits, making it particularly beneficial for retirees who rely on interest income for their expenses.

Example:

If Mr. Kapoor, a senior citizen, earns ₹60,000 as interest from his fixed deposits, he can claim a deduction of ₹50,000 under **Section 80TTB**, leaving only ₹10,000 as taxable income.

15.6 Section 24: Deduction for Home Loan Interest

Section 24 allows for a deduction on the **interest paid on home loans**. This deduction is available for both **self-occupied** and **rented properties**.

Key Features:

- For a **self-occupied property**, you can claim a deduction of up to **₹2 lakh** on the interest paid during the financial year.
- For a **rented property**, there is **no upper limit** on the interest deduction.
- You can also claim a deduction for the **interest paid during the pre-construction period** (before the house is ready for occupancy). This interest can be claimed in five equal installments starting from the year the construction is completed.

Example:
If Ramesh is paying ₹3 lakh annually as home loan interest for a self-occupied property, he can claim a maximum deduction of ₹2 lakh under **Section 24**, and the remaining ₹1 lakh will not be deductible.

15.7 Section 80G: Deduction for Donations to Charitable Organizations

Section 80G allows for deductions on **donations made to approved charitable institutions** and

relief funds. The deduction can be claimed for contributions to:

- National relief funds (e.g., **Prime Minister's Relief Fund, PM CARES Fund**).
- Charitable trusts, NGOs, and institutions involved in welfare activities.

Key Features:

- Donations are eligible for either **50% or 100% deduction**, depending on the organization.
- In some cases, the deduction is capped at **10% of your gross total income**, but donations to specific funds like the **PM CARES Fund** are eligible for a full deduction with no cap.

Example:
If Anita donates ₹50,000 to an eligible charity and the deduction is 50%, she can claim ₹25,000 as a deduction under **Section 80G**.

15.8 Section 80GGC: Deduction for Donations to Political Parties

Section 80GGC provides a deduction for contributions made to **political parties**. Donations made to any registered political party or electoral trust are eligible for a deduction.

Key Features:

- There is **no upper limit** on the amount that can be deducted.
- The donation must be made in a form other than cash (i.e., by cheque, demand draft, or electronic means).

Example:
If Raghavdonates ₹1 lakh to a political party, he can claim the full ₹1 lakh as a deduction under **Section 80GGC**.

15.9 Section 80DD: Deduction for Expenses on Dependent with Disability

Section 80DD allows a deduction for taxpayers who are taking care of a **dependent with a disability**. The dependent can be a spouse, child, parent, or sibling of the taxpayer.

Key Features:

- For dependents with **40% to 80% disability**, the maximum deduction is **₹75,000**.
- For dependents with **more than 80% disability**, the maximum deduction is **₹1.25 lakh**.
- The deduction is available for expenses related to medical treatment, rehabilitation, and training.

15.10 Section 80DDB: Deduction for Medical Treatment of Specified Diseases

Section 80DDB allows for a deduction on expenses incurred for the treatment of **specified diseases**, including cancer, neurological disorders, and chronic kidney disease.

Key Features:

- For individuals under 60 years of age, the maximum deduction is ₹**40,000**.
- For senior citizens (aged 60 years or above), the maximum deduction is ₹**1 lakh**.

Example:
If Mrs. Rao, a senior citizen, incurs ₹80,000 in medical expenses for treating a specified disease, she can claim a deduction of ₹80,000 under **Section 80DDB**.

Conclusion

While **Section 80C** covers the bulk of tax-saving options, there are many other deductions available under the Income Tax Act that can significantly reduce your taxable income. From health insurance and education loans to donations and home loan interest, these additional deductions help ease your tax burden and promote financial planning.

In the next chapter, we'll dive into **Tax Deducted at Source (TDS) Explained**, helping readers understand how TDS works, how to claim credit for it, and avoid common mistakes.

Tax Deducted at Source (TDS)

TDS Demystified

16.1 Introduction to Tax Deducted at Source (TDS)

Tax Deducted at Source (TDS) is a mechanism where tax is deducted at the point of income generation, whether it's from salary, interest, rent, or other payments. The payer (such as your employer or bank) deducts the tax before making the payment and deposits it with the government on your behalf. TDS ensures a regular inflow of tax revenue to the government and helps prevent tax evasion by collecting taxes at the source of income.

In this chapter, we'll explain how TDS works, when it is applicable, and how you can claim TDS credit when filing your income tax return.

16.2 How TDS Works

The **TDS mechanism** applies to various types of income, such as salaries, interest on fixed deposits, rent, professional fees, and dividends. The person making the payment (referred to as the **deductor**) deducts a percentage of the payment as tax and deposits it with the government.

Key Points:

- The person or entity deducting the tax is responsible for remitting the deducted amount to the Income Tax Department.
- TDS is deducted based on pre-determined **TDS rates** specified by the Income Tax Act.
- The person receiving the income (referred to as the **deductee**) is entitled to **TDS credit**. This means the amount deducted as TDS is adjusted against the total tax payable when filing the income tax return (ITR).

16.3 Common Types of Income Subject to TDS

TDS applies to a wide range of income sources. Here are some common income types where TDS is deducted:

1. Salary Income

- **Employer** deducts TDS on your salary based on your annual income and applicable income tax slabs.
- The deduction takes into account **tax exemptions** like HRA, and deductions like **80C** and **80D**.
- The TDS deducted from salary is reflected in **Form 16**, which is issued by your employer at the end of the financial year.

2. Interest Income from Fixed Deposits (FDs)

- **Banks** deduct TDS on interest earned from fixed deposits if the total interest exceeds ₹40,000 in a financial year (₹50,000 for senior citizens).
- The applicable TDS rate is **10%** if the PAN is provided. If not, TDS is deducted at **20%**.

3. Rent

- If you rent out a property to a business or individual (and the rent exceeds ₹2.4 lakh per year), the payer is required to deduct TDS at the rate of **10%** on rent payments.

4. Professional and Freelance Income

- Payments to professionals or freelancers are subject to TDS at a rate of **10%** on any payment exceeding ₹30,000 in a financial year.

5. Dividend Income

- Companies deduct **TDS at 10%** on dividends if the dividend income exceeds ₹5,000 in a financial year.

6. Other Types of Income

- TDS is also applicable on **commissions, interest on securities, contract**

payments, **insurance commissions**, and more.

16.4 TDS Rates and Threshold Limits

TDS rates and the threshold limits (minimum income for which TDS is applicable) are prescribed by the Income Tax Act. These rates and limits vary based on the nature of the income. Here's a quick overview of some key TDS rates:

Income Type	TDS Rate	Threshold Limit
Salary	Slab rates	Based on taxable income
Interest on Fixed Deposits (FD)	10%	₹40,000 (₹50,000 for senior citizens)
Rent on Property	10%	₹2.4 lakh annually
Professional/Consultant Fees	10%	₹30,000 annually
Dividend Income	10%	₹5,000 annually
Commission (non-insurance)	5%	₹15,000 annually
Sale of Property	1%	₹50 lakh or more

If you are earning income that exceeds these limits, the payer will deduct TDS at the specified rate and deposit it with the government on your behalf.

16.5 How to Claim TDS Credit

If TDS has been deducted from your income, you can claim credit for the amount when filing your income tax return. Here's how you can claim TDS credit:

Step 1: Check Your Form 26AS

Your **Form 26AS** is a tax credit statement that shows all the TDS deducted from your income and deposited with the government. It's important to regularly check **Form 26AS** to ensure that all TDS deductions have been correctly credited to your PAN.

Step 2: File Your ITR

While filing your **Income Tax Return (ITR)**, report the total income earned (including the income from which TDS has been deducted) and claim the TDS as a credit. The total tax payable will be adjusted with the TDS already deducted, reducing your tax liability.

Step 3: Adjust Refunds or Pay Additional Tax

- If the **TDS deducted** is more than your total tax liability, you are entitled to a **refund** of the excess amount. The refund will be credited to your bank account after the return is processed.

- If the **TDS deducted** is less than your total tax liability, you will need to **pay the balance** tax amount at the time of filing your ITR.

16.6 TDS Refund Process

If the TDS deducted from your income is more than your actual tax liability, you can claim a refund by filing your ITR. The refund process typically works as follows:

- Once you file your ITR and claim the refund, the Income Tax Department will process your return and verify the refund claim.
- If your refund claim is approved, the refund amount will be directly credited to your **bank account** within a few weeks or months, depending on processing times.
- You can check the status of your refund online through the Income Tax Department's **e-filing portal**.

16.7 Form 16 and Form 16A: Your TDS Certificates

To help taxpayers keep track of the TDS deducted from their income, deductors are required to issue **TDS certificates**:

- **Form 16**: Issued by your employer, this certificate shows the TDS deducted on your salary income. It also provides details of your salary, exemptions, and deductions.
- **Form 16A**: Issued for other types of income (like interest, professional fees, etc.), this form shows the TDS deducted on those income streams. Banks and other entities that deduct TDS issue this form to taxpayers.

Always cross-check the TDS certificates with **Form 26AS** to ensure that the details match and that you receive the correct credit for the TDS deducted.

16.8 Avoiding Common Mistakes in TDS

Here are some common mistakes related to TDS that you should avoid to ensure your tax liability is correctly calculated:

1. Not Linking PAN with the Deductor

Ensure that you have provided your **PAN** to the entity deducting TDS (such as your employer or bank). If your PAN is not linked, TDS will be deducted at a higher rate (usually **20%** instead of the standard 10% for most income types).

2. Failing to Check Form 26AS

It's crucial to regularly check **Form 26AS** for any discrepancies. If the TDS deducted is not reflected in Form 26AS, you will not be able to claim the credit. If you notice discrepancies, contact the deductor immediately to resolve the issue.

3. Forgetting to Claim TDS Credit

When filing your ITR, ensure that you **claim credit** for the TDS already deducted. Failing to do so could result in paying excess tax or missing out on a potential refund.

4. Overlooking TDS on Multiple Income Streams

If you earn income from multiple sources (such as salary, interest, and rent), make sure to account for all TDS deductions across these income streams. You should consolidate all sources of income and TDS credits while filing your ITR.

Conclusion

Tax Deducted at Source (TDS) is an important mechanism to ensure that taxes are collected at the point of income generation. Understanding how TDS works and regularly checking **Form 26AS** will help you stay on top of your tax obligations. When filing your ITR, claiming the correct TDS credit can ensure that you don't pay more tax than necessary, and if applicable, it will help you claim refunds efficiently.

In the next chapter, we'll discuss the **Income Tax Return (ITR) Filing Process**, taking you through each step to ensure accurate and timely tax filing.

The Income Tax Return (ITR) Filing Process

A Step-by-Step Guide to Your ITR

17.1 Introduction to Filing Income Tax Returns (ITR)

Filing your **Income Tax Return (ITR)** is a mandatory obligation if your income exceeds the basic exemption limit. The ITR serves as a record of your income, deductions, and tax paid or payable. Filing your return ensures that your taxes are calculated correctly, refunds are processed, and you stay compliant with the tax laws. In this chapter, we'll walk through the step-by-step process of filing an ITR, the documents you need, and how to avoid errors.

17.2 Who Needs to File an ITR?

You must file an income tax return if your income exceeds the basic exemption limit. The limits for **FY 2023-24** are:

- **₹2.5 lakh** for individuals below 60 years of age.
- **₹3 lakh** for senior citizens (aged 60 to 79).
- **₹5 lakh** for super senior citizens (aged 80 and above).

Additionally, filing is mandatory if you:

- Want to claim a **refund** of excess TDS.
- Have made **capital gains** during the year.
- Own **foreign assets** or earn foreign income.
- Spend over ₹2 lakh on foreign travel or ₹1 lakh on electricity in a year.

17.3 Types of ITR Forms

There are different types of ITR forms available based on your income source and category. Here's a quick overview:

ITR Form	Applicable For
ITR-1 (Sahaj)	Individuals with income up to ₹50 lakh from salary, pension, or house property.
ITR-2	Individuals with income from salary, capital gains, or more than one house property.
ITR-3	Individuals who have income from business or profession.
ITR-4 (Sugam)	Individuals who opt for the presumptive taxation scheme (e.g., small business owners or freelancers).

ITR Form Applicable For

ITR-5, 6, 7 For firms, companies, trusts, and other institutions.

Choosing the Right Form:

It's important to choose the correct ITR form based on your income sources. Filing the wrong form could result in penalties or a delay in processing your return.

17.4 Documents Required for Filing ITR

Before you begin filing your ITR, gather all the necessary documents to ensure accurate reporting. Here's a list of the key documents you'll need:

1. Form 16

Form 16 is a TDS certificate issued by your employer that details the tax deducted from your salary and your overall income for the financial year.

2. Form 16A/16B

For other income sources like interest from fixed deposits or rental income, you'll receive Form 16A or 16B, which shows the TDS deducted on that income.

3. Bank Statements and Interest Certificates

Gather your **bank account statements** and **interest certificates** for interest earned on savings accounts, fixed deposits, or recurring deposits.

4. Form 26AS

Form 26AS is your consolidated tax statement showing all the tax deducted on your income by various deductors (employers, banks, etc.) and the TDS deposited with the government.

5. Investment Proofs

If you've made investments to claim deductions under **Section 80C**, **80D**, or other sections, keep all relevant proofs (like PPF passbook, insurance receipts, etc.) ready.

6. Home Loan Certificates

If you've taken a **home loan**, keep the loan statement or interest certificate from the bank to claim deductions under **Section 24** for interest and **80C** for principal repayment.

7. Capital Gains Statements

If you've sold assets like property, shares, or mutual funds, keep records of the **purchase and sale**

transactions and details of the capital gains (short-term or long-term).

17.5 Step-by-Step Guide to Filing ITR

Follow these steps to file your income tax return easily and accurately:

Step 1: Register/Log In to the Income Tax E-filing Portal

Go to the official **Income Tax Department E-filing Portal** (www.incometax.gov.in) and log in using your **PAN**. If you're a new user, you'll need to register first.

Step 2: Choose the Appropriate ITR Form

Based on your income sources, select the correct **ITR form**. If you have salary income and your total income is under ₹50 lakh, you can use **ITR-1**. If you have capital gains or multiple sources of income, you may need to use **ITR-2** or **ITR-3**.

Step 3: Pre-Fill Your Information

The e-filing portal allows you to **pre-fill your personal details** and income information from **Form 26AS**. Verify the pre-filled data, and make any necessary corrections or additions.

Step 4: Enter Income Details

Enter the details of your income from all sources:

- **Salary** (as per **Form 16**).
- **House property income** (including rent received or interest paid on a home loan).
- **Capital gains** (if any).
- **Interest income** from bank accounts, fixed deposits, etc.

Step 5: Claim Deductions

Claim deductions under the relevant sections (such as **Section 80C, 80D**, and others). Ensure that the total deductions are within the allowable limits and supported by valid proofs.

Step 6: Compute Total Tax Payable

Once you've entered all the income details and deductions, the portal will automatically compute your total taxable income and the tax payable based on the applicable **income tax slabs**.

Step 7: Pay Any Additional Tax (If Required)

If your total tax payable exceeds the **TDS already deducted**, you'll need to pay the balance amount through **challan ITNS 280** on the portal. Once the payment is made, enter the **challan details** in your ITR.

Step 8: Verify and Submit Your ITR

After reviewing the return for accuracy, submit it online. Once submitted, you'll need to verify your ITR within **120 days**. You can verify it:

- **Electronically (e-verify)** using Aadhaar OTP, net banking, or other online methods.
- Or by sending a signed copy of the **ITR-V acknowledgment** to the Centralized Processing Center (CPC), Bengaluru, via post.

17.6 How to Track Your ITR Status

Once your return is submitted and verified, you can track its status through the e-filing portal:

1. Log in to the **Income Tax E-filing Portal**.
2. Go to the **Dashboard** and check the status under "Returns" or "Forms".
3. You'll be able to see whether your return is under process, successfully processed, or if any action is required.

17.7 Filing ITR Offline for Senior Citizens

Super senior citizens (80 years or above) who prefer not to file their ITR electronically can opt for offline filing. They can submit a **physical paper return** to the Income Tax Department by visiting the nearest **Income Tax Office**.

17.8 Common Mistakes to Avoid When Filing ITR

To avoid delays and potential penalties, ensure you avoid the following common mistakes:

1. Choosing the Wrong ITR Form

Choosing the wrong ITR form may lead to rejection of your return. Make sure you select the correct form based on your income sources.

2. Not Reporting All Sources of Income

Ensure that you report all your income, including **interest income**, **capital gains**, and **rental income**. Failure to disclose all sources may lead to notices or penalties from the tax department.

3. Ignoring Form 26AS

Always cross-check the TDS reflected in **Form 26AS** to ensure all the tax deducted has been properly credited to your PAN. Any discrepancy should be addressed before filing the return.

4. Forgetting to E-Verify

Your return is not considered valid unless it is **verified**. Failing to e-verify within the 120-day period will result in your return being treated as **not filed**.

5. Missing Out on Deductions

Ensure that you claim all eligible deductions, such as those under **Section 80C, 80D**, and others. Missing out on these deductions can increase your tax liability unnecessarily.

Conclusion

Filing your **Income Tax Return (ITR)** is a straightforward process if you follow the correct steps, gather the necessary documents, and avoid common mistakes. By filing your return on time, claiming the right deductions, and ensuring all income is properly reported, you can minimize your tax liability and ensure compliance with tax laws.

About the Authors

CA Lokesh Agarwal

Professional Overview: CA. Lokesh Agarwal is a practicing Chartered Accountant and Partner at "Agarwal A Kumar and Associates". With a strong foundation in the fields of Income Tax and Internal Audits, he brings a unique blend of traditional accounting expertise and modern technology solutions to his clients. He holds qualifications as a Chartered Accountant (ICA) and DISA (ISA), showcasing his commitment to continuous professional development.

Speaking Engagements and Webinars: Apart from being a Faculty at Guwahati Branch of ICAI, Lokesh is an active speaker at ICAI Guwahati, where he has delivered talks on the use of AI in CA offices, Power BI and other technologies. Additionally, he conducts Monthly webinars focusing on improving office productivity through the use of AI and modern technology. He has done 15+ career counseling sessions over whole of Assam in various schools, colleges and universities

Core Areas of Expertise: Lokesh's key areas of expertise include Income Tax, Internal Audit, Cost optimization and proficiency in tools such as Tally Prime, Excel, PowerPoint, and ChatGPT. His focus on integrating technology into daily operations helps clients optimize their workflows and achieve higher productivity.

YouTube Channel: TechFlow Hub by Lokesh: In an effort to spread knowledge and empower the CA community and All offices at large, Lokesh runs a YouTube channel called TechFlow Hub by Lokesh.

Awards and Achievements: Lokesh's dedication to technology and innovation was recognized when he became the Runners-up in the AI Hackathon organized by EIRC of ICAI. He was also the Semi-Finalist at the National Levels Competition on AI in ICAI showcasing use cases of AI at work applications.

Trainer and Educator: As a passionate trainer, Lokesh offers courses and workshops on Excel, Macros, and ChatGPT. His training sessions are designed to help professionals and businesses enhance their technical skills, streamline processes, and increase overall efficiency.

He has also initiated to teach application of Technology at work, for Free where he holds Online Classes and anyone wishing to learn can join the groups. Special session on demands of the members are also taken up by him so that technology adoption becomes a General and Natural thing without any hindrance.

About the Authors

CA Shekhar Agarwal

CA Shekhar, Agarwal a practicing Chartered Accountant hailing from Tezpur, Assam, stands as an inspiration to many. Born on 30th July 1991, he has carved an impressive path through his life, setting a remarkable example of self-reliance and commitment to the community.

Shekhar's journey began in Don Bosco High School, Tezpur, where he laid the foundation for his academic success. In 2011, he emerged as a state topper, securing the 9th rank in the Higher Secondary (HS) Exam. This was only the first of his many academic accolades.

His academic prowess led him to Gauhati University, where he pursued a Bachelor's degree in Commerce. Not surprisingly, Shekhar graduated as a university topper in his major, reflecting his unwavering dedication to his studies.

However, his most notable accomplishment came in 2016 when he passed the Chartered Accountant Exam. It is worth noting that Shekhar achieved this feat without any external coaching. His success was a result of his unfaltering belief in self-study and determination. He became one of the few students who managed to clear the exam through self-study, a testament to his grit and perseverance.

But Shekhar's achievements are not just limited to his academic and professional life. He embodies the true spirit of philanthropy. After passing his matriculation exam, he began teaching underprivileged children. His teaching fees were used to fund his studies and complete his Chartered Accountancy (CA) Course. He achieved his goals without seeking any external financial assistance from his parents or others, truly embodying the spirit of self-reliance.

Today, Shekhar continues to contribute to society. He still offers free academic assistance to underprivileged children. Moreover, he has taken it upon himself to spread financial literacy throughout Assam. He tirelessly works to bring knowledge to every corner of the villages in Assam, ensuring that everyone has access to basic financial education.

CA Shekhar's story is a shining example of what one can achieve with determination, self-reliance, and a robust belief in giving back to the community. His journey continues to inspire many, reminding us all the power of education and the importance of community service.

www.ingramcontent.com/pod-product-compliance
Lightning Source LLC
Chambersburg PA
CBHW021542150726
47990CB00006B/2353